ROLLING ROCKS DOWNHILL

How to Ship YOUR Software Projects
On Time, Every Time

CLARKE CHING

ISBN: 1505446511
ISBN-13: 978-1505446517

ACKNOWLEDGMENTS

I must start by thanking Winnie Manning, my very tolerant and loving wife. You are right, Winnie: I am very lucky.

I had a lot of support and encouragement along the way. This book wouldn't be here without the concepts and principles I learned from Eli Goldratt and the many members of the Theory of Constraints community. I also thank Ken Schwaber, Mary Poppendieck, Tom Poppendieck, Johanna Rothman, Tom Gilb and David J. Anderson, who got me into Agile and Lean Software Development. I've made many Agile friends along the way and several have become true friends: Greg Brougham, Dr. Bruce Scharlau, Ali Law, Graeme Thomas, Chris McDermott, Gillian Julius, Kevin Rutherford and the utterly magnificent Rob Lally.

And finally, there's no way this book would be here if Jim Bowles, my TOC mentor and friend, hadn't taken me under his wing and taught me just a tiny bit of what he knew. You changed my life Jim, and thank you!

FOREWORD

You've seen this movie before. You're on a project. You've been told to work faster, better, and cheaper. No more "pick two out of three." No. You need to deliver all three out of three. Especially the faster part.

Maybe one of your teammates or someone in management has the bright idea that maybe transitioning to agile or lean will help. Maybe it does in some small way. But, it's not enough. You're on a death march, iteration by iteration. Or, with your board, you can see that you are making progress, but you're not working "fast enough."

Or, you're not delivering what your customers need. You're still trying to "do it all." Why? Because it takes you forever to release anything.

You know there's another piece to this. You just don't know what.

You need to read Clarke Ching's *Rolling Rocks Downhill.*

Clarke delivers the goods with this business novel. You can see how Steve, our hero, learns about small batches, reducing work in progress, and bottlenecks. You can see how management's typical "motivations," such as management by objectives, doesn't work in a team-based complex adaptive system, such as a software project.

Learn how Steve, a middle manager, who is part of the dysfunctional system, learns about small batch sizes, work in progress, and bottlenecks. He slowly learns what they do wrong. He makes changes slowly—just as you would in real life. The teams learn how to change slowly, just as they would in real life.

His management doesn't understand what's going on. They alternately threaten and reinforce his efforts. I see this occur all the time. The teams are so tired of working the old way, they are ready to try anything, because they can't stand the idea of another death march project and being blamed for failure.

And, because you see all of this, you will root for the team's success, as I did. You'll understand the mutiny, when the project manager pushes the team one too many times. And, if you have not seen the magic of how agile, lean and Theory of Constraints can actually work in organizations, you might be surprised when the team pulls off the "impossible."

You might think this is impossible, or because it's a business novel, this is fiction. It's not. I've seen and coached normal people, on normal teams, working normal hours, as they transition to working in this way, complete projects again and again. Clarke shows you the secret sauce.

Do you want a way out of your insanity? Is it time for you to learn how to take control of your projects, and learn how you can release a product your customers want, when you want to release it, a product that works?

You can. Read Clarke's *Rolling Rocks Downhill.* You will have many "aha" moments. You will say, "Now I get it!" This book will change how you look at projects and what you think you can do about the predicament you are in.

Use the ideas here. Don't start another death march project. If you find yourself in another impossible project, where your management wants it "faster, better, cheaper," use this book. You will limit your work in progress, make your chunks of work small, and find your bottlenecks (to name just three of the tools) to make your project possible, instead of impossible. You don't need to be extraordinary. You need to be diligent.

Have fun reading. I did.

Johanna Rothman, author of Jolt Productivity award-winning *Manage It! Your Guide to Modern, Pragmatic Project Management*

Arlington, Massachusetts

Friday, August 3rd

CHAPTER ONE

I love the smell of jet lag first thing in the morning. It smells of bacon and eggs and comes with the best-tasting coffee in the world. The bacon comes from across the water in Belfast. The eggs, though, are grown locally in Watt's Bridge, and they're cooked by Luca, whose Dad moved to Scotland from Italy after the Second World War, opening first a fish and chip shop and then later the deli and cafe where I sat, my brain craving Luca's espresso. Step one in my three-step jet lag recovery program.

Luca slid up to my table, leaned over and gently placed a glass of cold water and an espresso cup in front of me. "Steve, my friend, where are you back from *this time*?"

"Singapore," I said. "Another technology conference."

He tut-tutted, as if he disapproved of all my air miles, or my work-life balance. Or, more likely, both. I was a regular early-morning customer. "You want your usual?" he asked.

I said, "Yes, please," and he slipped away.

I looked around the room as I sipped coffee. Three of the dozen tables were occupied by nightshift staff from nearby Watt's Bridge Hospital. Two police officers sat at another, their radios chattering in the background, and a half dozen cab drivers crowded two tables near the windows, watching over their cars in the rank outside. The walls were covered in black-and-white framed pictures of the "old country."

And then my mobile rang.

I glanced at its screen. Phil McDermott, my chief programmer and best friend since I was thirteen. It was 5:26 a.m. Phil had never been a morning person. Very strange.

I answered. "You okay?"

"You're back from Singapore today, right? I got the date right didn't I?"

"Yeah, what's wrong?"

"You're in Luca's, for breakfast?"

"Yep. What's up?"

"I'll be there in about two minutes. I've got bad news, Steve. Can you order me breakfast? Please. And coffee. Lots of coffee."

He hung up.

I turned and spied Luca standing behind the large, stainless steel and glass counter. He was writing the lunch specials on a chalk-board. He saw me looking, rushed over and said my breakfast was less than a minute away.

"Can you cook me up another breakfast, same order? Phil's joining me. And I'll need a couple more double espressos."

He paused, glanced across at the table of taxi drivers, and then smiled to himself. "I'll have both plates ready in one minute."

A moment later, the cafe door's bell jingled and Phil shuffled in, dressed in jeans and a green T-shirt. Phil is tall and thin, and has—for as long as I could recall—looked like a bald, malnourished ver-sion of Paul McCartney. He's just a year older than me, but he looks much older. I still have some hair. He spotted me, nodded, and started walking to my table. He walked awkwardly, as if he was auditioning to be an extra in a zombie movie, and I wondered if maybe he'd hurt himself.

He sat, and I smelled the stink of stale cigarettes and alcohol.

"Whoa," I said. "Late night. Have you been home yet?"

"I grabbed a couple of hours sleep, but I needed to talk to you. I knew you'd be here."

Before he could tell me what was so urgent, Luca arrived with two fully-loaded plates, two small cups of his special black tar and two glasses of cold water. He told Phil he didn't look so good. Phil nodded—there was no denying it. I picked up a slice of crispy ba-con, folded it into my mouth and savored its salty, fatty goodness. Bacon was step two of my jet lag recovery program.

"It's perfect. Thank you."

Luca grinned and tilted his head towards the cabbies. "Thank them. Your need seemed greater." Then he left us alone with our food.

Phil splashed a little water into his espresso to cool it and then drank it in one gulp. He looked at mine, asked, "Are you drinking that?" then grabbed my cup and chugged it down too.

He shook his face like a dog shaking water from itself after a swim. "I learned something last night in the pub that you're not going to like. It's bad."

Bad? Phil looked at life the way a cat looks at spilled milk. He talked me into my three-step jet lag tradition, reasoning that jet lag was unavoidable for a guy with my ambition. If I'm going to be awake at 4 a.m., with no chance of sleep, why not be eating bacon?

If Phil said something was bad, it probably was.

"Go on."

"We were out for a few pre-wedding drinks," he said. Two of our mainframe operators were getting married later that week, and a lot of my colleagues had taken vacation time to help celebrate. "Pauline and Kevin Jones traveled up from Birmingham."

Pauline had worked with us for years, but then, just over a year earlier, she and her husband moved south to look after his aging mother.

"Some time around midnight," he continued, "we were drinking shots and Pauline—you know her, she never could hold her drink—let it slip that her mother-in-law wasn't as sick as they'd let on when they left."

"What do you mean?"

"She was poached by Chaste Group, Steve, to go work on a no-frills version of our FPP."

FPP stood for the Future Perfect Project. It was our top-secret, software-intensive, project, or it had been, anyway. We were building a brand new financial product for richer, older people. Before Pauline moved south she had been the project's lead analyst. She'd kindly delayed her departure until just after our requirements work was complete, to minimize the hassle she'd said. And now, apparently, she was working for Chaste Group.

"Chaste? Are you sure?"

"Yup."

Chaste Group had a reputation for cherry-picking the easy money from established markets: credit cards, long-distance telephone calls, airlines, car rentals ... the list goes on. Phil and I, on the other hand, worked for Wyxcomb Financials, a.k.a. Wyx-Fin, which was part of the multi-national conglomerate, the Wyxcomb Group—or just Group, as we called them—and we built big, sturdy, grown-up products.

I smiled. "You sure she wasn't just having a little fun with you? Teasing you?"

He shook his head, then looked down glumly at his (my) empty coffee cup.

"They're copycatting a product that doesn't exist yet?"

"They're even launching on April 1st, so they can piggyback off our advertising campaign for free."

I winced. That little detail made Pauline's story sound more plausible. The press loved a good angle, and they'd no doubt run a bunch of David and Goliath stories casting us as the bad guy and giving Chaste free advertising.

"Hang on ... does Pauline still think we're delivering in April?"

He shrugged. "She must, and I didn't tell her otherwise."

I watched Phil's eyes, waiting for it to click. He was a coder. He coded at work during his days so he could pay his bills, he wrote open-source software in his evenings and weekends for fun, he even took his laptop on vacation with him ... to code. He didn't pick up immediately on the schedule implications.

His head jolted up. "She doesn't know we're running late ..." I let him process a little more. "Chaste will beat us to market."

I thought out loud. "Their product will be smaller, that's the way they do things, but it'll still appeal to sixty, maybe eighty percent of our market. A smaller product is quicker and cheaper to build."

Phil nodded. "Especially when you steal your competitor's lead analyst right after all the hard thinking has been done."

I let out my breath slowly. "Does anyone else know?"

"No. I doubt Pauline even remembers telling me. She'd had a lot to drink by then."

"Good." I thought a moment, formulating a plan. "Why don't you go home, grab some sleep, and I'll handle it from here. You should enjoy the rest of your vacation day."

"Sure thing." He smiled, though he didn't look happy. "But not until I've finished my breakfast. You're paying right? So, did you enjoy your junket?"

"The conference was good." It had been sponsored by a vendor, so they'd paid my expenses. I had given a presentation about our use of one of their products.

"Your talk?"

"My presentation," I said, enjoying the banter with my friend, "was very well-received. I won an award."

He raised an eyebrow. "For what?"

"Runner-up for best presentation."

"Runner-up? Impressive. Did you get a statue?"

I wrinkled my nose at his friendly sarcasm.

"You found time to work on your tan," he continued.

"Networking."

Phil frowned, confused. To him, networking meant routers and IP addresses. Then he got it. "Golf ..."

I smiled.

Phil stretched his arms and yawned. "You know, we will sort out FPP. No matter what our customer reps say, the specs still have fat we can trim. We can cut features, and there are a number of processes we *could* automate, but don't need to. No one will like what we deliver, but yeah, we'll find a way to do it."

"Yeah. Somehow."

He'd gained a little color in his face, but he still looked tired and hungover, and malnourished. He also, I realized, looked sad.

I said, "I'm surprised at Pauline. I didn't think she was the sort of person who would do something like that."

"She was a friend."

I grimaced. I didn't know what else to say. We finished our food in silence, then I offered to drive Phil home.

He declined, saying that he'd be fine. Which in a way was a relief, since I was eager to start the third step in my jet lag recovery routine: working, interruption-free, in my office. Normally I'd use that time to get a head start on the admin that built up while I was away, but that day I had something better to get on with: rescuing the most important project I'd ever worked on.

Phil said, "Later, then, dude," and left.

The *dude* was, in case you're wondering, ironic.

CHAPTER TWO

I made my way to my office in Wyx-Fin's HQ, just off the Watt Bridge High Street. It was 6:05 a.m. when I sat down, and as predicted, the floor was empty and would be for most likely another hour.

My office sat in the prestigious sea-facing corner of the building. But since my department was relegated to the sixth floor, my sea view was blocked by a thoughtlessly placed parking garage. I docked my laptop, switched it on, and started to wrap my head around Phil's news while it booted up.

Wyxcomb Group had invested heavily in FPP. No one said it out loud, but it was one of those bet-the-farm investments you hear about; it was high risk, but if it paid off it was supposed to save our subsidiary. I wasn't privy to the numbers, but I knew one of our operating assumptions was that we would be first to market and would experience what our CEO called *First Mover Advantage*. So Phil's news was going to upset a lot of people.

I'd start the ball rolling by calling Eleanor Scharlau, our chief financial officer, who would only want to know one thing: Could we match Chaste's April date? I'd say we could, but at a cost. We'd have to slash the product again, refuse all change requests and work more overtime than was healthy. I'd advise against that, of course, and she'd say something about commercial realities forcing unpleasant compromises on us and we'd both end up agreeing we would match the April date, but she'd have to cough up more budget to cover the overtime. She'd then talk to Mark Richmond, chief marketing officer, and together they'd talk with our CEO, Halifax Gibbet, who'd hem and haw for a few days before realizing he had no choice but to inform his masters in Group HQ, in Malmö, Sweden, that we were no longer the only horse in this race. Or something like that.

Before I spoke to Eleanor, though, I needed to get my story straight. I opened FPP's latest status reports and checked that nothing significant had changed while I was in Singapore. I looked first at the internal FPP status report—the one freely available on our internal network to any staff who were interested—and, as I expected, it said the project was progressing on schedule, moving towards an April 1st launch. It described that date as aggressive but achievable, which was our code for *This date isn't really feasible, but we need to keep the pressure on our staff, otherwise they'll slack off.* I then opened the latest management-eyes-only update, which stated we were tracking towards a launch well after April, probably around October or November.

So nothing had changed. April 1st was nine months away, but as the project stood we were predicting we would need at least six months more than that. If we wanted to launch on April 1st for real, then the product needed some serious pruning.

I glanced at my laptop's clock and noted it had switched from Singapore to local time. Normally it would be too early to call anyone, but this phone call was forgivable. I dialed Eleanor.

She answered immediately. "Steven. This is early. What's up?"

When I first started working for Eleanor, we'd quickly come to a working arrangement. First, she told me, I was the computer guy and she was the accountant, so as long as I didn't ask her too much about accounting then she promised not to ask me too much about computers. Second, she liked to manage by exception, so I had a free rein. We'd never discussed the third point, but I'd very quickly figured it out myself: She didn't like people or small talk all that much.

I skipped the small talk and broke Phil's news to her.

"Can we beat them?"

I skipped the negotiation, too. "Yes, I believe so, but it'll be very, very tight. We'll have to make the usual compromises."

"Of course we will," she said, cutting me off and clearly not wanting to hear any details. "Come up and see me sometime ..."

she went quiet for a moment, "around noon. That'll give me time to start lowering everyone's expectations."

She hung up, and I opened my calendar and cancelled all of that day's meetings, making room for my attack.

CHAPTER THREE

I stepped out of the elevator into the penthouse foyer at 11:52 a.m. The security guys buzzed me straight through into the executive reception. Eleanor's personal assistant, Brittany, greeted me with a well-rehearsed smile, informed me that Eleanor would see me as soon as she could, then asked me to take a seat. I picked the leather couch closest to Eleanor's office and half-heartedly perused that week's *Economist* while I waited.

Ten minutes later, Eleanor's door flew open and Halifax Gibbet, the man himself, our CEO and savior, five foot six inches tall (and, some said, round, though no one had ever been brave enough to try and measure him), stomped out, barking over his shoulder: "No more excuses!" He slammed the door then marched straight past me and down the corridor to his office. I couldn't tell if he deliberately ignored me or if he hadn't even bothered to ignore me. Whichever it was, he ignored me.

A moment later, Eleanor's door opened again and Mark Richmond, our chief marketing officer and FPP's sponsor, sauntered out of Eleanor's office. I heard him say: "Can you get back to me by, say, four?" Eleanor replied: "Five" from inside her office. Mark, a tall, fit man with pitch-black hair, had been well-known across Scotland a couple of decades earlier when he played on the Scottish Rugby team. He closed Eleanor's door and saw me sitting on the couch. Smiling broadly, he said, "Nice tan, Steve," then strolled across the hall to his office.

Twenty-five minutes later, Eleanor came out and—although I don't think I was technically sleeping, just resting deeply—startled me awake with a sharp "Steven."

I stood and we shook hands formally, as was her way. As she led me into her office, I noticed that she left her office door wide open, which I took as a good sign. She pointed me towards her couch, a short-legged, luxurious, antique thing (not unlike its owner), and like a good doggie, I sat. I felt awkward, as always, as I sank deep into the soft cushions, feeling my pants legs ride up and revealing not just my socks but a bit of leg as well. Eleanor sat down in a matching chair, her back straight, crossed her legs and got straight to the point.

"Hal and Mark tell me your new information confirms rumors they'd been hearing as well."

I rolled my eyes. What did she expect them to say? To admit they got caught with their pants down?

She let out a deep breath. "Truthfully, how healthy is the FPP project?"

I shrugged. "FPP is as healthy as any project of its size. Before today's news, we were on track to deliver before the end of next year."

"On track? What on earth does that mean?" She shook her head. "When were you actually going to deliver? Give me a month."

I put my hand up onto my chin and rubbed it, trying to give the impression I was thinking; which I was, but I wasn't thinking about when we'd deliver, I was thinking about how I could word my answer without causing Eleanor to react in a way that would make both of us regret her leaving her door open.

The truth was, we never knew when a project of this size would finish until we got a good bit into our testing phase. If we got lucky, finding few bugs during testing and not needing to make too many changes, then we would finish the testing phase quickly, with little rework. FPP hadn't yet started testing, so we estimated the testing phase would take approximately forty percent of the project's duration. The reality would depend on how lucky we got, and we didn't get lucky often.

Eleanor wanted a month, but the best I could give her was a season. "Autumn next year, if we got lucky. Though given the size and complexity of FPP, more likely winter."

"And the odds of it running into spring?"

I didn't know how to answer that, but I did my best. "One in six."

"So we were playing Russian roulette," she said, nodding slowly to herself. "Here's hoping you're firing blanks."

I said nothing.

"So FPP would have, most likely, delivered twelve to eighteen months from now."

I smiled weakly. None of this was news to her.

"Well, now you've got seven months."

"Pardon?" April 1st was just under nine months away.

"Hal promised Group we would beat Chaste to market. Our new launch date is February 1st."

I raised my voice. "I agreed to match them, not beat them."

"Steven," she hissed, shushing me and pointing towards the open door. "We have no choice."

I lowered my voice, as instructed. "He's robbed us of two months. He can't do that."

"He can, and—in fact—he just has." She spoke quietly, coldly. "The date isn't open for debate. But if you're as clever as you think you are, young Steven, Hal and I are confident you will find a way."

I stared at her, aghast and angry. My mind raced ahead. April 1st would have been tight, but I believed we could trim FPP of enough fat—lower value features and processes—to be able to do it. But there's only so much functionality you can slash before the product is no longer commercially viable. There's only so much overtime we can work before people burn out. It was too late to bring new people onto the project. That'd just slow everyone else down. The other option, the one I knew we'd end up exercising no matter how much I hated it, was to cut our quality standards back even more than we usually did.

I thought a moment. February 1st didn't make sense. Very few customers would buy the product until after the new tax year started in April.

I said, "How many customers does Mark expect to buy the product in February and March?"

"A dozen or so per week." She shrugged. "It doesn't matter. He won't actively promote the product until April."

"Then why launch in February?"

"Because that's the promise Hal made. You don't need to know more than that."

I nodded, though I wasn't happy since I'd be the one who got blamed if we ran late. "So, if things get desperate, could we launch with spreadsheets to buy us a few weeks, then launch the actual software solution in April? Those two extra months could make a huge difference."

She looked at me as if I were an idiot. I took that as a no. Smoke and mirrors clearly weren't good enough.

I said, "We might not make February. We need a Plan B."

She glanced at the open door as she considered my comment. I thought she looked like she wanted to tell me more, but couldn't.

She spoke very deliberately. "Halifax promised our masters in Group two things: First, and clearly foremost, that he will beat Chaste to market and we will be selling FPP to real customers, albeit on a small scale, on February 1st. Second, we will be selling FPP on scale, in April, as customer demand grows after the new financial year. He promised he would deliver, or else."

She left the *or else* hanging there, as if she were inviting me to ask her about it. I obliged. "Or else?"

"You figure it out."

It wasn't difficult. No one said it, but everyone knew Hal's job was on the line. FPP was the rabbit up his sleeve, his get-out-of-jail-free card and his rescue plan all rolled into one. The Wyxcomb Group had been pumping cash into us for the last three years. They described it as investing for growth, but really, for all the growth they'd seen so far (exactly none), they were keeping us afloat. FPP was not only the rabbit up Halifax's sleeve, but also his future cash cow. No rabbit, no cow; no cash, no job. No job, no shirt on his back. No shirt, no sleeves, nowhere to hide his rabbit. Or something like that. Maybe the analogy makes more sense with top hats.

"Just because Hal's job is on the line doesn't mean we can just magically deliver FPP any earlier."

"I know."

We both sat there, silent for a few moments while we contemplated the position we had suddenly found ourselves in. I searched for a bright side, and the best I could come up with is that Hal may well shaft us, but at least I'd get a mention in his memoirs.

Eleanor broke the silence. "You will ship something on February 1st, correct?"

"Is Mark on board? If his team doesn't slash the product's scope back enormously then we're dead."

She nodded. "Yes, but Catherine doesn't know yet." Catherine worked for Mark. He was FPP's sponsor; she was our primary customer representative.

"Our overtime budget will soar."

"Of course."

I sighed. "Our product will launch prematurely. It will be buggy as hell and we'll spend months and months after launch nursing it into good health, fixing it. You won't get any new features for months."

She shrugged. "I know how these things work, Steve."

I nodded slowly. Our negotiations were over and I'd done my part as best as I could. I'd objected to the date and explained the consequences, and that was all I could do. I hated it, my staff would hate it, and our customers wouldn't like our product, but I'd done my job.

"Okay."

"Good," she said, then smiled. "Now, when you leave my office, you need to leave with a beaming smile on your face. As far as you are concerned, February 1st is not only achievable, but it's just the sort of kick in the pants your guys needed all along, and Hal is a good man for providing it. Understand?"

I forced the smile onto my face, just to show I could do it. "Of course I do. We've been in tighter situations and survived."

"Good lad," she said. "Now, one last question."

I raised my eyebrows.

She glanced towards her door to check that the coast was clear before she spoke. "Tell me, who normally gets blamed when a software-intensive initiative like FPP fails? The CEO, the CFO or the IT guys?"

CHAPTER FOUR

I left Eleanor and took the stairs down to my office, closed the door behind me and pulled the blinds. I had twenty minutes before FPP's weekly management meeting started, and I needed to clear my head. I sat there and stared blankly out my window at the parking garage.

Suddenly I jerked awake. I glanced around the room, trying to figure out which room, in which country, I was in. I was disappointed when I realized where I was. I checked the time. I'd slept for only a few minutes.

I tried to shake the sleep out of my head. I'd been awake a long time, and I had a long day ahead of me with just a few minutes until FPP's meeting. I took a deep breath and braced myself before I made the hardest call of the day: my mom.

I needed to call her and tell her there was a chance I might not be home for dinner.

So here's the awkward bit, what people referred to as *Steve's Personal Circumstances*: My mom had lived with me and my two girls ever since my wife, Fran, passed away two-and-a-half years earlier. We had been vacationing in Rome—we'd only been married three years, and our girls were still very young then—when Fran suffered a brain aneurism. It was sudden. It was quick. I still don't recall much of the days, or weeks, that followed. Mom flew to Rome and helped me sort things out, then took early retirement and moved in with us. She has been looking after us since.

When I told her I'd be late, she said, "Oh, Steven. The kids haven't even seen you yet. I'd put them on the phone, but they're both over at Isabella's house right now."

"I know. I'm sorry," I said, then quickly moved on, not wanting to have that conversation yet again. "Can you get them their dinner, too? I'll try to be home in time to put them to bed."

"I suppose so," she sounded disappointed. "What's wrong this time?"

I started to tell her Phil's news, but she interrupted me before I got far.

"Pauline? Short? Mousey hair? A bit dumpy?"

I agreed, though her description was harsh.

She snorted. "I never liked that woman."

"You only met her twice."

"Yes. But I didn't like her either time."

"She was a friend," I said quietly.

"I don't imagine, then, that she betrayed you lightly."

Thinking of Pauline made my stomach clench, so I quickly filled her in with the rest of the story. She pretended she didn't understand all the modern-computer-talk, but I knew she knew much more than she let on.

"My poor boy," she said. "You've all worked so long on this project."

"It'll be okay." I said I'd call her later and I'd try my hardest to get home in time to see the kids before their dinner, but I couldn't guarantee it.

"Steven, they haven't seen you in nearly two weeks."

I winced. As a rule, whenever I had an urgent work situation I'd still go home and have dinner with the girls before putting them to bed. Then I'd either work from home or return to the office. But I knew I was too jet-lagged to work late and that I had a long day ahead of me.

"This is urgent, Mom. I *will* be home in time to put them to bed."

"I know you will."

We said our goodbyes, and I put down the phone and looked out my office windows. It was raining heavily outside, which didn't help my mood. I never expected to be living with my mom in my early forties, and she never expected to be living with me, playing mother to her grandchildren. We were both still trying to figure it out.

I watched as, one after the other, plump raindrops rolled down the outside of my office window.

Drip. Drip. Drip.

Gravity sucks.

I picked up my phone. I had time for one call before FPP's management meeting started.

CHAPTER FIVE

I dialed my other boss—my dotted-line boss—Norbert Billings, the Wyxcomb Group CIO. Norbert was tall, blonde and Dutch, and he had worked within the company ever since the company he had been working for was acquired by Wyxcomb decades earlier. He answered after a couple of rings, and I gave him a quick update on the FPP situation. He said he'd already heard the news. He offered no direction or advice, only a request that I keep him up to date.

We talked for another fifteen minutes or so about the conference (he congratulated me on my award) and other initiatives I was working on for him—stuff that affected all software development activity across the Wyxcomb Group and not just within Wyxcomb Financials, the subsidiary I was working for.

Then Norbert blindsided me. "Now, tell me, did you ever contact Craig Lally?"

Craig Lally worked somewhere upstairs in our TCQ team (our snappy acronym for Total Customer Quality). Every Wyxcomb site had a TCQ team that did training and consulting on whatever the Group's latest quality initiatives were. Months earlier, Norbert had asked me and my counterparts in the Group's other subsidiaries to meet with our local TCQ team to explore how we could use *Best Practice Quality Practices* within our development teams.

Norbert's gift, if you could call it that, was his ability to regul toss Idea Grenades over the wall. If we acted on every one o grenades, we'd be so busy *improving* we'd have no time left to do any work. More to the point, I knew someone in Wyxcomb Health had contacted this Craig Lally fellow, and they'd ended up outsourcing their entire development team. I did not want to be outsourced.

I'd never met Craig and I wasn't in a rush to do so now.

I said, "No. Not yet. We've been particularly busy lately."

"Funny, your colleagues in the other subsidiaries have been particularly busy too. Did you, at least, read the report he wrote up about his Wyx-Health work?"

"Ahhh, no, not fully, not yet." I could see it poking out from near the bottom of a pile among the other clutter of my desk.

"Craig strikes me as being a very thoughtful man ..."

I said, "I am sure he is ..."

I heard him breathe out slowly. "I want you to call him and I want you to meet him. You work in the same building, for heaven's sakes. The Health guys called him and they are based in another country. You know Steve, even you might learn something."

Even me? Sometimes working for Norbert felt like being nibbled to death by ducklings. A little nip here—*You don't ask for enough help*; a little nip there—*Have you read this report?* None of the nips hurt individually, but over time ...

"Yeah. I know. You're right," I said out loud, trying to sound suitably respectful while saying *nip, nip, nip* in my head. "I'll call him. But FPP's management meeting starts in a few minutes. I really have to go."

"Okay," he said. I thought I heard him sigh, and I felt bad.

We ended the call, agreeing that we'd talk more the following week when I was in Malmö. I glanced at the edge of Craig Lally's Wyx-Health report and chose to ignore it, for now, at least. The last thing I needed was a bunch of manufacturing guys who'd lost their jobs because their factories had been closed down trying to help me. I pushed my chair back from my desk and headed out the door.

I had a very important meeting to gate-crash, a bunch of IT professionals to fire up, and a metaphoric rug to pull out from under them.

CHAPTER SIX

I sat at the head of the sixth-floor conference room table. I was a few minutes early for the FPP weekly management meeting. The first to arrive. The conference room looked like it came straight out of an up-market 1990s conference room catalog: large oval wooden table, wooden cupboards at the back of the room, dark brown carpet. But it was also fitted with a few modern features. Whiteboards, a wired-in PC at the front of the room, and a projector and screen helped usher the room into the millennium.

I whiled away the minutes twiddling my thumbs and looking out the window, admiring the castle perched atop Castle Peak, one of the city's two intrusive crags. The castle looked formidable against its backdrop of dark rain clouds. I grew bored with the castle very quickly—you've seen one, you've seen 'em all—and turn my attention back inside the building where I spied a large potted palm tree sitting just inside the conference room door. I studied the palm for just a couple of seconds before I came up with a plan: I would hide behind it, then jump out and surprise people as they came into the meeting. My kids would have loved that. I smiled at the thought but left it at that; I'd save my surprise for later in the meeting.

A few minutes later, Phil arrived. He'd showered and shaved since I last saw him, and he looked tired but presentable.

I said, "Aren't you on vacation time?"

He shrugged. "Some things are more important."

Shortly after that, Gregor, FPP's project manager, burst into the room lugging an old photocopy paper box. Gregor was a big, scary-looking guy, barrel chested with a military-style haircut. If he had a personal life, he'd never mentioned it. Office rumor had it that he slept with the lights on; not because he was scared of the dark, but because the dark was scared of him. You wouldn't call him a people-person, but he was a solid manager. Solid enough that I had entrusted him with FPP, Wyx-Fin's biggest project in living memory.

His eyebrows shot up when he saw me sitting at the head of the table. I wouldn't normally attend a meeting like this one, so I said this seemed a quick way to catch up with my most important project. He'd forgive my lie when he knew the real reason.

Gregor sat at the other end of the table and placed the box on an empty chair beside him. We made idle chit-chat as he removed a stack of plastic folders and stapled papers from the box, then neatly sorted them and arranged them into piles. The rest of his team slowly dribbled in one by one. Vrinda, the lead analyst; Tim Phillips, the testing manager; and Catherine MacDonald, FPP's customer rep. I greeted each as they arrived and they congratulated me on my award. Word spread fast—and whether that was good on not depended on the news.

Catherine said, "Mark texted me. He said you have some news?"

Speaking of news. "Later."

I felt awkward. Catherine and Pauline used to lunch together, and I thought they might have been friends outside of work, before Pauline moved south. Before she betrayed us. My news was going to sting.

Gregor kicked off the meeting at five past the hour, as was unofficially standard at Wyx-Fin. He picked up one of the piles of paper, kept the top sheet for himself and passed one half of the stack to his left and the other to his right. I ended up with a stack of spare sheets at my end of the table. I pick one up and glanced at the heading. It was the agenda.

"Item one," said Gregor, "is to review the project status." I checked the agenda, and he was indeed correct. No one would accuse Gregor of having agenda issues.

He picked up one of the larger stacks of paper, split it, then passed stapled copies around the table. It was FPP's Gantt chart, showing the project's detailed schedule.

Gregor summed up for me, "As you can see, Steve, everything is progressing on, or close to, schedule. We have just under three months left of the development phase before we start integration testing."

I zoned out as Gregor worked through the plan, line by line, in his nasal monotone, and read through it without his guidance. I kept one ear open, just in case, listening for anything interesting. The analysis, design and coding phases of the project's Gantt chart took up the first half dozen pages. I turned quickly to the last two pages, which showed the remaining coding tasks and then the integration testing which was scheduled to start in a few months. Following that, we'd start the first of what could be several phases of testing.

I flipped back to the first page and then scanned the entire plan, my finger tracing the shape as I took it all in. The project was progressing to schedule, but that didn't mean we'd ship on April first. I knew we wouldn't. Gregor knew we wouldn't. Everyone else in the room suspected we wouldn't. We couldn't know for sure until we started testing.

That was how we motivated people: by keeping the pressure on. It didn't actually work, because we almost always delivered late anyway, but I hated to think how late we'd deliver if we took the pressure off.

I tuned back into Gregor's update. "Development work is continuing on for the income projection statement and the audit history viewer. Both tasks require another six weeks' work each."

"I still don't understand how come we're doing them at all?" asked Vrinda, the lead analyst on FPP and a long-time friend. She had dark hair and was tall and athletically built. That day she wore a dress suit. She never minced her words, but sometimes I thought she might have achieved more if she had. "They're low priority but they're taking up twelve weeks' of effort from two of our strongest developers. It's a complete waste of time."

Gregor's face pinched, as if in pain. He let out a long, dismissive sigh. "For goodness sake, Vrinda, do we have to do this every time? Both of these features were important enough to survive March's descoping exercise so they cannot, by definition, be low priority. We will build them."

"But ..." Vrinda protested.

"But nothing. They're in the scope. That's it. The project doesn't finish until they're finished. End of story."

He glared at her, holding her gaze until she blinked then grumbled agreement.

I zoned out once again and let Gregor work his way through the plan. As I waited, I studied the palm once more. There were three of them in this room and dozens of other plants spread throughout our office. Our facilities department hired those plants from a local company called Lease-A-Plant. I guess someone in accounts described it as *outsourcing their green capability*, or something like that. The first time I heard their name mentioned, I thought they were talking about a person named Lisa Plant—who I imagined was aging rock star Robert Plant's daughter.

Gregor eventually finished and asked if there were any comments. When there weren't, he glanced at me, no doubt wondering what I was really doing there, and said, "Right. Next up then, we have thirteen change requests."

He distributed another pile of papers. I took one copy but put it to the side. I didn't want to know the details. I already knew what would happen next: arguments.

"Only three pages today?" asked Phil, sarcastically.

Gregor frowned. "We should get through them in twenty to thirty minutes."

"Good," said Phil, "because I'm too tired for this today."

Gregor looked at the first page then frowned some more.

He looked towards Catherine then to me. "I spoke to Catherine earlier, and she has already agreed to close CR 315."

Catherine was a petite woman with long, deliberately wild, red hair. She looked around the table with what I took to be an apologetic face. "I didn't realize it would require CORETRAN changes. There's a manual workaround."

Catherine was a star. At the start of the project, Mark Richmond had asked me what one thing I needed from him, as FPP's sponsor, to ensure its success. I answered immediately: a top-notch customer—someone who could provide our development staff with good quality, timely decisions; someone Mark could comfortably delegate big decisions to so that he didn't become a bottleneck; someone who wouldn't be intimidated by a bunch of techies when they started speaking jargon. Mark's a sharp cookie, and a few days later Catherine turned up in the FPP workspace carrying six boxes of up-market donuts.

CORETRAN was the opposite of a star, whatever that is. A planet, perhaps? (It certainly was a pain in Uranus.) It's our oldest software systems and, as you can guess from the first part of its name, it sat at the core of our software solution. It was hard to change CORETRAN. It always had a big line of work waiting to be done to it, and over the years we'd all learned that the one rule with CORETRAN work was to avoid it if at all possible.

Gregor sighed, again. "I'm horribly disappointed to see the next change request. It's number 191, Customer Level Income. What's happening, guys? We rejected this over six months ago and now it has been reopened. Can someone explain, please?"

I watched as Vrinda took a deep breath, then glanced across at Catherine and Phil before speaking.

"I reopened it, Gregor. We originally rejected it because, at seventy-seven days' work, it was too expensive. But Phil and I took a closer look at it last week, answered a few outstanding questions, and we think it will now only take ten to twenty days."

"I asked them to," added Catherine. "This is a very important change. It simplifies the product, making it both easier to sell and to service. If we were to write the requirements again, this would be right up near the top of the list."

"But, Catherine, it wasn't included in the original requirements. Not even hinted at," said Gregor. "You can't just make up features as you go along."

"We wouldn't have asked for it if it weren't important." She looked at me and smiled. "You guys make us go through so many administrative hoops for each change that we only ever ask for the most important."

Gregor shook his head. "Nonetheless, I am rejecting it. If we do it then we risk delaying the integration work."

"Could we swap it for something?" suggested Catherine. "There are several other features I would happily drop if it meant we could get this approved."

Vrinda said, "The audit functionality we just discussed, for instance."

"We can't do that," said Gregor. "Colin is already halfway through the work, and I'm not throwing away good work. I'm sorry, but the best I can do is add it to the phase two wish list. How's that?"

Catherine and Vrinda looked at each other, shrugged, then nodded in defeat. We all knew the odds of phase two ever happening on any project were low, but they were even lower on a project that was already running late.

I saw Gregor put a large *X* next to the change request. There were plenty more to come.

I glanced at the clock on the wall. I didn't need—or want—to hear any more. I knew what would happen next: Gregor would protect his budget and delivery date; Catherine would protect her product; some requests would be approved; many would be rejected; others would be approved with a watered-down solution. It wasn't pretty, but what could you do?

I smiled to myself as Gregor tidied the papers in front of him. He asked if anyone had any further questions. No one did, so he turned to me and asked if I had any questions.

I said, "No, but I have some news."

CHAPTER SEVEN

Vrinda reacted instantly. "Oh great! Here we go again. Another arbitrary date imposed on us from on high. Just what we need."

Catherine's response was slower and came in phases. At first she was far more controlled than Vrinda. I saw her flinch when she heard about the betrayal, but then, almost instantly, she assumed a poker face. "So, the only way we can possibly hit the date is by throwing away most of the work we've done? And lowering our quality standards?"

I said, "Something's gotta give."

She looked at Phil. "Pauline really did this?"

He nodded.

Catherine lowered her gaze towards the table. "I do not know what to say."

Vrinda reached across and patted Catherine on the back of her hand. "This really sucks."

Catherine jerked her head up and looked directly at me. "I bet she justified her betrayal by saying it wasn't personal, it was just business."

I nodded. It sure felt personal.

I gave everyone a few minutes more to react to the new information, to vent. I also knew they understood the February 1st date was, effectively, set in stone so there was no point bitching about it.

I was tired and I needed them to get on with things.

"I've booked this conference room for the rest of today and all of tomorrow. I'll leave shortly and then return at four p.m. tomorrow. When I return I want you, Gregor, to present me with a detailed recovery plan to deliver the first release of FPP in just over twenty-four weeks' time. Okay?"

Gregor said, "Of course," and everyone else nodded.

I nodded back. "I want you all to keep four things in mind."

"First, you have to deliver a complete, saleable product on this date. It's not just a software development problem. Marketing have to do their stuff. And Catherine, I know you know this, but you need to set up your call center and rollout the product across the entire organization by February 1st."

Catherine nodded, still looking a bit shell-shocked.

"Second. We cannot deliver eight months' work in six months. You will have to cut the product drastically. Catherine, your job here as customer rep is to ensure the product has the features necessary and sufficient to go live, but no more. Gregor, your job is to ensure we meet the date. We cannot and will not miss the February deadline.

"Third, you all know this is Wyx-Fin's number-one priority project. If anything gets in your way, then tell me and I'll move it. Gregor, I'll need a list on Friday. Plan your schedule accordingly.

"And finally, I hate to say this, but quality is negotiable—to a point. This baby will be born premature. The delivery will be difficult and we will have to nurse it into good health long after February 1st."

I looked at Tim. "We will ship a shoddy product, but I cannot tolerate a dangerous product. I need you to adopt a risk-based approach to your testing."

I turned to Catherine. "And Catherine, come February 1st, the product will contain a large number of known and unknown defects. We will do our best, but you or Mark will need to make the final call about whether we go live or not. Okay?"

Her forehead furrowed as she considered the implications. She clearly wasn't happy, but what choice did she have?

"Okay," she said. At least she now had plenty to focus on besides Pauline's betrayal.

"Good," I said. I pushed my chair back from the table, then put on my grandest voice. "This conference room is officially a War Room."

CHAPTER EIGHT

I got back to my desk feeling desperately tired, but quite pleased with myself. Norbert was right: I loved fighting fires. But when I looked down at my computer screen and saw a little yellow While-you-were-out sticky stuck to it, all my energy disappeared.

While I was out, Craig Lally had called. He wanted me to call him back.

The note said URGENT.

Another little nip from Norbert.

I screwed up the note, dropped it in the trash and turned my mind to more important things.

I started by looking up the meaning of the word petulant. It meant what I thought it meant. Then I sorted through my emails again, and then I spent a little time with our salary reviews. At 4:50 p.m., I dropped by the conference room (War Room) and glanced through the window. I noted plenty of activity and returned to my desk without interrupting the team. Then I ran out of excuses.

I fired up the internal phone directory and searched for Lally.

There was only one Lally, and his job title was "Flow Master." What the hell is a flow master? Was Craig one of the janitorial staff?

No. Judging by his desk location—which was a corner office above mine high enough to have a genuine sea view—he was way higher up the Wyx-Fin food chain that I was. I clicked through to his Wyxcomb intranet resume. It read like a buzzword bingo card: Lean, Six Sigma, TOC, and a whole bunch of other acronyms I didn't understand. No MBA, nor anything similar, but loads of manufacturing experience and—going way back—a half dozen patents to his name.

I noted that Craig was his middle name. His full name was Alistair Craig Lally. Made sense. Who'd take someone called Ali Lally seriously?

I pulled on my headset then reluctantly dialed his number, hoping *petulantly* that he had already left for the day.

An irritatingly chirpy male voice answered the phone. "Craig here."

He sounded older than I was; in his fifties, at least, but who could tell for sure over the phone.

I gritted my teeth, wondered if maybe I should not have made this call while I was chronically jet-lagged. Then I figured it was maybe just a few seconds too late to be asking such a question. I introduced myself.

"Steve. Thank you so much for calling me back. I'm very much looking forward to working with you."

He said Norbert had briefed him about my situation earlier in the day, and since his diary was atypically empty that week, he figured it was as good a time as any for us to catch up.

I should, he said with unrestrained enthusiasm, just name the time and he'd name the place.

Not so fast.

"Before we talk, I need to know what you did at Wyxcomb Health."

He replied with clearly diminished enthusiasm and a good bit less chirp. "I helped them figure out how to make more money, more happier customers, and happier staff. That's my job."

"You outsourced them," I said flatly.

The line went quiet for a moment.

"Is that why you didn't contact me earlier in the year, when Norbert suggested?" he asked quietly. "You think I want to outsource your department?"

I held my breath for a moment before answering. "Outsourcing is the last thing I want to happen to me or my team. The last thing."

"I understand. In that case, you should know that I did not outsource them, Steve. They chose, with my assistance, to replace their hand-cranked, custom-built software, which frankly was on its last legs, with a software package. That was their choice."

Oh come on. "That's the same thing, said with nicer words. They now pay someone else to build their software and a Wyx-Fin development team is without a job."

"True-ish. And they made their choice and they're very happy with it. I advised them, but I didn't force them to do anything other than think a lot and occasionally listen to some new ideas."

"Yeah, but ..."

"But nothing, Steve." He was getting snappy. "Norbert warned me you'd find any excuse not to talk with me, that you weren't the sort to ask for help. Would you like to hear the full story before you judge me?"

My jaw tightened. He didn't pull his punches and I couldn't disobey my boss's direct instruction. I rolled my chair back from my desk, the headset cable following me, and put my feet up on the corner of my desk.

"Sure, sorry, go for it." Though truthfully, I wasn't one bit sorry.

"Gladly. Wyxcomb Health asked me to help them figure out how to deliver projects on time. They said that their biggest problem was that they were spending a huge amount of time and money finding and fixing defects at the end of each project. They said this was common across your industry. Sound familiar?

"Uh-huh. Our standard development methodology finishes with a testing phase."

"And you do more than just test during that phase?"

"Well, obviously we fix any defects we find when we are testing."

"That's what the health team said too. They said their *test phase* should actually be called the *rework phase.* They said it was an incredibly inefficient and unpredictable way to build software, but they had no idea how to work any differently. Sound familiar?"

I kept my voice neutral, unhappy that he was correct. "Yes."

"Now, Steve, I've worked most my life in manufacturing and I've never written a line of software code in my life, but when I heard about the long rework phase I suspected I could help them. I've solved that particular problem many, many times before, though not in software development.

"You thought they could get rid of their testing phase?"

"Get rid of it, or reduce its duration enormously. Have you ever worked in a factory, Steve?"

"No."

"Well, imagine for a moment you're standing in an old-fashioned car factory, somewhere in the industrial midlands, in say the 1970s or 80s, before the Japanese quality movement hit the Western world. I'm sure you've seen pictures on TV. The factory builds cars in two distinct phases. In the first phase they build the car. Then, in the second phase, they find and fix the multitude of defects created during the first phase. If it helps you could picture a bunch of serious-looking men wearing white coats and carrying rubber mallets which they use to beat dents out of the newly-built cars."

I could picture it. I'd driven one of those cars, second-hand, as a teenager. I was never any good mechanically, but my friends were. I couldn't have afforded to own the car otherwise.

Craig went on. "We call this way of working *late-inspection*, though that name is a little deceptive because late-inspection is fine provided nothing needs fixing. Japanese manufacturers figured out how to build quality into their products during phase one, skip phase two, and ship their products directly to their retails. Much faster. Much cheaper. Much better product, and with far fewer warranty problems. Most Western manufacturers learned from the Japanese and work that way nowadays.

"I had hoped to help Wyx-Health's software development team figure out how to build quality in, but we soon realized they had a problem far bigger than their development methods. They called it their Camel Problem."

The question was begging to be asked, so I asked it, "Did it have something to do with straw?"

"Indeed it did. Their software and hardware were like an old, overloaded camel nervously watching as day after day its owners loaded it with more and more straw. It ran on an outdated technology platform that hadn't been formally supported by its vendor for over six years, and the code was buggy and difficult to change without making things worse. Things were so bad, they'd stopped selling their products to new customers. They were terrified the entire system would collapse due to increased volumes."

I said I understood. Wyxcomb Health weren't the first to be

crippled by an antiquated, brittle software system. The first project I'd ever managed was at Wyx-Fin Bank, where I replaced a similarly crippled check-processing system. We'd done that in house, though; we hadn't needed to outsource it.

"So they shot the camel and bought a newer, better camel instead?"

He chuckled, and I thought I heard him slap his hand on his desk. "Exactly."

I said, "Okay, Wyxcomb Health had to replace their software—I understand that. But why'd they buy new software? Why not build their own? Surely it would have been cheaper?"

"That's a fair question with a simple answer. We ran the numbers and it was indisputably more profitable for them to buy rather than build."

I shook my head and started waving my hands in the air as I talked into the headset.

"No. No way. That doesn't sound right. Short term, maybe, yes, it might look cheaper, but not in the long run."

He listened as I elaborated that, in my experience, the upfront costs of buying a software package might sometimes appear cheaper, but that Wyxcomb Health people surely couldn't have taken into account the longer term costs of ownership: the annual fees, the extortionate costs for custom work, the overhead of having to upgrade whenever the vendor issued a new release. And so on.

"Oh, it wasn't the cheaper option, Steve. It was the more profitable option. I'm not paid to save money, though that's often a nice side-effect. I'm paid to help the Wyxcomb Group make more money."

Huh? "What's the difference?"

"The difference, in this case, was millions of pounds. It would have taken twelve to twenty-four months to rewrite their existing system. It took less than three months to install the first tranche of the new package, and a month after that, Wyx-Fin retail branches started selling new Wyxcomb Health branded products. With all the extra revenue bought in, the project paid for itself within three months of launching.

He asked me if I understood. I said I did. But that didn't mean I liked it.

He said, "The Wyxcomb Health business couldn't afford to wait for the internal software development team to rewrite their system;

they would have lost millions in sales. Like I said, we ran the numbers. Millions. Commercially and technically speaking, this was a good decision.

I heard what he was saying, but it still wasn't the full story. I gave it one more shot. "But buying a healthcare package limited them to selling more-or-less the same product as their competitors."

He said, "True, but in this case Health's products are commodities. No matter how they, or their competitors, dress themselves up in fancy marketing clothing, the only substantial difference between the products in this market came down to branding and scale. Wyx-Fin Health's new products sell well because we have a respected brand and a branch network spread across Europe, which has aggressively cross-sold the product to existing customers.

"And if I may pre-empt your next two objections. Wyxcomb Health pay their vendor significantly more than the internal IT team used to cost, but their fees are directly proportionate to the number of our customers using their system. We negotiated it that way. What's good for us is good for them. What's good for them is good for us. You'd be surprised how motivated they are to keep enhancing their product. The more we sell, the more money they make; the more money they make, the more they can afford to enhance their product. It's what we call a virtuous circle."

"Win-win?" I said, trotting out the old cliché.

"Yes, indeed," he said. "Plus, you'll be pleased to know that Wyx-Fin Health's internal IT team kept their jobs. They're busy learning the new package and figuring out how to migrate their existing customers to it. They like their jobs now, much more than they did a year ago. They're looking forward to ridding their lives of the camel. So, really, it's win-win-win."

He stopped talking and I found myself in the awkward position of not being able to argue with him. "That's interesting, but I still have no interest in outsourcing my team."

"I should imagine you wouldn't. Is your software also like the broken old camel? Norbert didn't seem to think it was."

I said, "No, of course not." Which wasn't quite true. Some of it was, but most wasn't.

"Good," he said. "Where and when, then, shall we meet?"

"Give me a minute." I figured he'd assume I was checking my diary, but really, I was checking my pulse.

The fight—and the petulance—had all gone out of me. Craig had dangled the bait in front of my nose. I'd gobbled it up and I quite liked the taste. I wasn't hooked, but I did want to meet him in person, to perhaps hear a little more. But, equally, I didn't want to be part of anyone's experiment. And that, without a doubt, was why Craig wanted to "help" me. He needed a guinea pig.

But that wasn't all. I just hated that Norbert had forced me to make this call. I hated being nagged. It was some stupid teenage thing, I guess, that had never left me. Whenever I was nagged, my inclination, as foolish as it was, was to do the exact opposite.

After a little negotiation, we agreed to meet for a long brunch at ten on Tuesday morning the following week. At least I'd get some bacon out of this.

CHAPTER NINE

Finally, I was home. My house looks like a fairy tale from the outside, a two hundred-year-old stone gatehouse built into the defensive walls of a country estate, complete with vines creeping up the wall and round turrets. A couple of times each day, tourists who'd driven slightly off the beaten track would stop to take photographs. From the inside, though, it looks much like any modern small house, although the walls are made of stone and much thicker than normal and the doors were built for a time when people were considerably shorter, which required a lot of ducking from me. We'd extended off the back of the house a few years earlier, before the kids arrived, but you couldn't see the extension from the front.

I parked my car and snuck through the front door as quietly as I could so I could surprise the kids. I heard Scooby-Doo playing in the den at the far end of the house (the TV series, I assumed, not the cartoon dog himself come to life). I dropped my bag in the doorway, slipped my shoes off, then tiptoed down the hall with my coat pockets rustling. I smiled to myself, imagining how my two girls would react when I surprised them with their gifts—and me. They loved surprises.

I snuck through the house then paused at the doorway, peering through the partially open door at my family. I smiled, though I still felt a stab of guilt at not making the time to get home sooner. Mom, elegantly dressed, as always, had the girls fed, bathed and in their pajamas. She was combing Alison's blonde hair while Ashley, the eldest, lay on the mat with a coloring book and pile of colored pencils in front of her. One of our fat tabby cats, Mr. Purrrrple, snuggled up beside her cleaning his paws. Ashley's tongue stuck out the side of her mouth as she concentrated.

I pushed the door open. "Ahoy, me mateys!"

"Dad!" They both rushed to me, and moments later I was covered in hugs and they were covered in kisses. Then their minds turned to other business.

"Did you bring us any presents? Did you? Did you?"

I sat the girls down and dished out the parcels. They were shiny, tacky little things—the gifts, not the girls—but they were just the sort of thing my two little girls loved.

It felt good to be properly home.

Friday, August 4th
FPP launch date - February 1st, next year

CHAPTER TEN

I returned to the FPP War Room at 3:55 the following afternoon, as agreed.

The walls were covered with flip chart paper and Post-it notes, the table with printouts and coffee cups. Gregor was busy typing, Vrinda was doing nothing in particular except looking grumpy, and Catherine wasn't there. Phil was busy snapping photographs of the walls using his phone. A stack of empty pizza boxes sat at the back of the room. Lunch or last night's dinner, I couldn't tell. I breathed in, and immediately wished I hadn't. If work had an odor, then I guess you could say the room smelled of work.

I placed a small box of cookies (made by Mom and the girls) on the table, then went to the far side of the room and forced open a couple of windows.

I asked Gregor if he had a plan.

He nodded. "It's aggressive but, I think, workable. We have some very busy months ahead of us, but we should make it."

I thought I saw Vrinda roll her eyes, but I wasn't sure.

Catherine returned and we all sat down. Gregor described how they'd come up with their plan. He said they'd started with the spreadsheet produced during their last descoping exercise earlier in the year. The spreadsheet listed all FPP's features and ranked them as must-haves, should-haves, could-haves and won't-have features. I'd always suspected Catherine had deliberately thrown in the won't-haves at the start of the project, so we'd have something to slash during the descoping exercise that almost always happened later on. At the end of the exercise last year, Catherine swore we'd cut every ounce of fat from her product, and some muscle as well.

Gregor snorted. "If that earlier exercise was a gentle descoping, then today's session was battlefield triage. We took far fewer prisoners this time, Steve."

Clearly pleased with the results, Gregor explained his triage approach. They had written every feature in the spreadsheet on its own little yellow sticky note, then scattered the dozens of sticky notes randomly across the breadth of the conference room's back wall. Then, they used a divide-and-conquer approach to force-rank every feature.

It went like this: Gregor had chosen one sticky note at random, the group had agreed it wasn't unusual in any way, and they placed it in the middle of the wall. Gregor called it the pivot feature—like on a set of old fashioned balancing scales. Then, one-by-one, they'd taken every other sticky note and asked if it was more or less valuable than the pivot feature. The more valuable features got moved to the left side of the wall, the less valuable to the right. The number of stickies wasn't evenly balanced, but that didn't matter. They repeated the process with the two halves until they'd ended up with the most important features, the must-must-haves, on the far left side of the wall, the must-haves sitting next to them, and so on.

Gregor said, "We paused at this stage to figure out what to do next. We concluded there must be some absolute bare minimum set of must-have features we needed before we can go live.

Catherine said, "I decided where that point was on the wall. We marked that point with the extra-large pink sticky note."

She pointed to the wall and I nodded, acknowledging the pink sticky note's presence.

"Okay." I went to the wall and scanned the sticky notes. They meant little to me—I didn't need to know the details in order to do my job—but I could see how, as I moved from left to right, the product built up feature-by-feature until it hit the pink sticky note. Even I could tell that the product truly was bare bones. Skeletal, even.

I was about to turn back to them when a horrible thought occurred to me. I looked around the room to see if there was another bunch of stickies. There wasn't.

I turned to Gregor. "There's no web work here."

He nodded, the corners of his mouth turning down even more than usual.

"You've descoped the web app?"

He nodded again.

I looked around the table, hoping one of my colleagues would burst out laughing at the little joke they'd played on me.

Silence.

I shook my head in disbelief. "Seriously? We're launching without a web app? People will laugh." I looked at Catherine. "Can we do that?"

She grimaced. "Yes, we can. We will look lame, but on the plus side, most sales will originate in our branches or, once we advertise, our call center."

I looked back at Gregor.

He said, "We don't have enough runway to launch with a web app by February."

I closed my eyes for a moment and took in a calming breath. "I'm so sorry, Catherine."

She shrugged. "It's not your fault, Steve. You didn't change the date. Circumstances did."

I turned to Gregor, and was pleased my voice stayed steady. That calming breath thing really works. "What did you do next?"

"Next," he said, "we developed a brand new project plan to build this bare minimum. We all agreed, by the way, that except for one exception which we will discuss later, it would slow us down if we tried to bring any new staff on to the project at this stage."

I nodded.

Gregor cleared his throat, as if he were about to make an announcement. "The new plan, to build up to the pink sticky, came in at just over fifteen weeks' work—most of it testing."

Catherine said, "If we went live with only the bare bones features, then our support processes would be a nightmare. We'd be better going live with spreadsheets. I needed those processes more than I needed a web app."

"I understand."

"So," Gregor said, "we added a few more really-really-should-have features until we had a plan that takes six months, including two weeks at the end for launch. Testing starts in five weeks."

I asked Catherine if she was happy with that.

"Happy? No. But what choice do I have?" She shook her head.

"If FPP were a tricycle, maybe it would have three wheels and handlebars. But no seat. It's going to be an uncomfortable ride, but I can live with it until February, so long as we add the seat after that, in phase two."

She was right to assume that Eleanor and Mark had money ferreted away to fund FPP until the end of the following year. So, yes, in theory she would get her phase two. But realistically, we'd spend much of phase two fixing the stuff we got wrong in phase one. I decided to let her figure that out in her own time.

I turned to Gregor. "Are you confident you can achieve the date?"

He didn't respond straightaway. I watched as his eyes seemed to search for the answers somewhere near the back of his head, then he straightened his back, took a deep breath, and said, "Steve, it's an aggressive schedule, but if you're happy to pay the overtime, then I am confident it is achievable."

"Good." That was the gung-ho attitude I liked to see.

He let a tiny smile sneak out. "I'll announce compulsory paid overtime on Monday and I'll ask everyone to voluntarily cancel any holidays they have planned for the next six months. If I don't get enough volunteers, I'll cancel vacations."

"They'll hate you for that," Vrinda snapped at him. She'd been silent so far, which was unusual for her.

Gregor snapped back. "You can't make an omelet without breaking a few eggs, Vrinda. You do the analysis; I'll do the managing. We'll both be a lot happier."

She grimaced. "Yeah, right. A lot happier."

I intervened. "Look. If you two kids can't play nicely together then I'll send you to your rooms."

My words were light-hearted, my tone was not. I couldn't have the team falling apart before we'd even restarted the project. I looked each of them in the eye and they both said sorry, though clearly neither meant it. I changed the topic.

"This is good work, everyone. I'm pleased with what you've done. Now, what do you guys need from me?"

Gregor said, "We identified three obstacles for you to remove."

He turned to Tim, who said, "The first is test data. Every project I've worked on here has been hobbled by the lack of good test data. "

I nodded. That was true.

"It's hard setting up test data," Tim continued. "You need a broad knowledge of our existing systems as well as knowledge of the new application. The people who have that knowledge are considered too valuable to spend their time creating test data. "

"What would you like me to do, Tim?" I asked.

"This is the area where we could add new staff to the project without slowing everyone else down. We'd like a dedicated team established to set up test data. We need the team to be overstaffed so that they respond quickly—in minutes rather than weeks—to requests for new data. And, I'd like them not to complain about it."

I smirked. He was doing well until the last sentence and he knew it. "I guarantee you that you'll have a dedicated, overstaffed team by the end of next week." I'd draw people in from the business, and Catherine and Mark would pull a few strings if need be. "But I can't guarantee they won't complain. I'm no miracle worker. What's the second obstacle?"

Gregor said, "Catherine and her team sit with us, and it's been great having them so close when we have questions or issues. But we'd also like to have other customers, such as the actuaries and a representative from the marketing and documents team, working directly with us. We'd also like some of the periphery IS teams moved in, too. In particular, we'd like at least two DBAs sitting here with us."

"Good thinking," I said. I tried, with every project, to work as one colocated team, but despite my good intentions, I almost always failed. But FPP was different. It was corporate priority number one. If anyone complained when I wanted to move them, I'd threaten them with a call from the personnel department. And if that didn't work, I'd threaten them with a personal call from Halifax Gibbet himself. "I'll get facilities on the transfers immediately. It'll be done by Wednesday."

"In that case," interrupted Phil enthusiastically, "can you get us an FPP team espresso machine—a good one? This automatic dispensing machine coffee gives me heartburn, the tea has stuff floating in it, and it has whitener in it, not milk. It's a health risk."

He was, of course, being flippant. I said, "Is that your third obstacle?"

"No," Gregor stepped in. "We need a large dedicated meeting room. This conference room would be ideal. And we need whiteboards, plenty of whiteboards. And a large stock of whiteboard marker pens; they're as rare as hens' teeth around here and I'd hate to lose this battle for want of a marker pen."

"Done." I told them that Carol, my PA, had spent most of the morning moving meetings around specifically to free up space.

"As of today, this conference room is dedicated to FPP, as are three smaller meeting rooms. I'll get Carol to check, each day, that the meeting rooms are fully stocked with pens and other stationary." Sometimes it's the small things that matter the most.

I straightened the papers in front of me then looked around the table, making certain to catch everyone's eye.

"Thanks, everyone. You've done good work these last two days." I stood. "And now I want you all to go home and enjoy your weekends. I'll see you all at Monday morning's team meeting."

As everyone stood, I caught Vrinda's eye and asked her quietly, "Can you walk with me?"

She glanced at Gregor. He was packing papers into boxes and didn't look in our direction.

Quietly—meekly, might be a better word—she said, "Yes."

CHAPTER ELEVEN

Vrinda and I had joined Wyx-Fin on the same day from the same graduate program. She was, in fact, only three weeks younger than me. Our first few years in Wyx-Fin, we rotated through different jobs as we went on what Wyxcomb Global HR called *Our Strengths Discovery*. In normal speak, we spent a few years finding out what we were good at. On a spectrum of thick-skinned-ness, I was at one end and she at the other. So she specialized in analysis and I in management. As an analyst, she removed ambiguity and uncertainty; as a manager, I figured out how to live with them both.

We'd been friends since meeting, and sometimes her kids and my kids played together on the weekends. Her husband once worked in Wyx-Fin as an actuary, but now was a moderately successful science-fiction writer.

We chatted idly as we walked to my office. *How are your kids? Fine, yours?* That sort of thing. When we reached my office, I closed my door and we sat.

"Is everything okay?"

"Yeah," she said, unconvincingly.

"Are you sure? In the meeting, you only spoke once and then, honestly, you seemed a bit snippy. What's up?"

She bit down on her upper lip, as if forcing herself to not speak, then blurted out, "Am I telling you this as a friend or as one of your staff?"

"A bit of both, I guess."

"In that case, I'll choose my words carefully." She paused a moment, then spoke. "That man is an arse. None of us like working for him. He doesn't listen. He doesn't trust any of us and frankly, we do not trust him."

I nodded, but said nothing. I didn't want to interrupt the flow. She kept talking for a good minute before she said something that forced me to interrupt.

"For months, he's been lying about the health of the project," she said.

"Lying?"

"He's painted a nice, rosy picture of the project to you and the steering group, but we all knew we'd never be live in April."

I nodded slowly, surprised at her naivety, and looked directly in her eyes to ensure I had her attention. "Gregor didn't lie to me or to our steering group. April was always an aggressive date."

She looked at me blankly. "You knew we'd run late?"

"Of course. And so did everyone on the steering group."

She blinked and looked at me as if I'd just told her the Tooth Fairy and the Easter Bunny were the same person. (They're not.) She was a great analyst, but after two decades in the game, where she'd seen project after project run late, she still managed to be surprised when it happened yet again.

"So why'd Gregor lie to us? Was it just to keep the pressure on? Is that it? Huh? Crack the whip to keep us lazy workers from slacking off?"

I felt myself getting a little angry. "Look, we wanted to ship in April, but we knew that date was aggressive. We kept the pressure on because if we didn't then we'd have no chance of delivering early."

She scrunched up her lips, thinking. "Did you ever consider that, given no one believed the date was feasible, perhaps some folks slowed down? No point flogging a dead horse? Especially when everyone thinks the jockey is a jerk. Who works hard for a jerk?"

I shrugged.

She shook her head. "Surely there are better ways to motivate us lazy workers?"

Instead of answering, I asked her a question. "Look, what

would have happened to scope if the date had been say, eight months later? December next year rather than April? Would the scope have been bigger or smaller?"

She looked up, thinking, I guess. "Bigger, of course. Catherine cut a lot of features to fit into April."

"And how about change requests? With more time up our sleeves would we have more or less change?"

"More, obviously."

She screwed up her nose, as if she smelled something bad but couldn't quite tell where it was coming from. Or maybe she could.

I said "You know this. The scope of the project always expands until it's too big to fit in the time available to deliver it. If we didn't put aggressive deadlines in place we'd never ship anything."

"I suppose."

I was ready to wrap this up and go home to see my kids. I changed the topic. "You look tired."

"I am," she said, then narrowed her gaze. "But, you know, I don't want your sympathy. I want you to fix FPP."

"How?"

Her mouth fell open. "How should I know? That's your job."

I shook my head. "No, that's not my job, that's Gregor's job. He manages the project's uncertainty. And you might not like him, but he is good at his job."

"But you're still crossing your fingers, right?"

"Pardon?"

"Just now, in our meeting, Gregor told you the February 1st date was 'aggressive but achievable.' Which is how you just described the April date. If it's aggressive then it's no slam dunk. We should expect it to run late, right?"

My jaw fell open just a little. I didn't know it at the time, but I was experiencing a stress reaction called cognitive dissonance, which happens when new information conflicts with one's established beliefs. Basically, my brain was flummoxed. The typical response to cognitive dissonance is not to take on the new information and try to work through the discrepancy, but to remove that stress by ignoring or discounting the new information. And that's exactly what I did.

I shrugged. I smiled. I glanced at my watch. I changed the subject. "Look, I've barely seen the kids since I got back."

I said I'd walk downstairs with her, if she liked. We did the we-should-catch-up-sometime-with-the-kids chat as we made our way out of the building, transitioning out of work mode and into friends and family mode.

We both swiped out at the front of the building then stood for a moment before we parted. Vrinda would turn right towards High Street and I would cross the foyer, then head down to the basement garage.

I said, "Look, I know you desperately want FPP to succeed. So do I. So does Gregor. But he has an incredibly difficult job juggling a lot of question marks and balancing a load of conflicting needs. I don't think he's the ogre you think he is."

She shook her head. "I never said he's an ogre. I said he's an arse, and I implied this project is going to crash and burn."

Monday, August 7th
FPP launch date - February 1st, next year

CHAPTER TWELVE

Monday morning at 10 a.m., Gregor announced the new plan at the FPP team's weekly meeting in our building's basement auditorium.

No one seemed surprised.

Some, mostly the younger folk, looked happy. Probably at the unexpected gift of some paid overtime coming up for Christmas. Most didn't.

I gave a little pep talk, casting Chaste Group as an unscrupulous enemy. I doubt it worked, but I felt better.

At 11 a.m. I met Ron McKnight, my support and maintenance manager. Ron is a grey-haired, Wyx-Fin old-timer, a curmudgeonly mix of gruff, grumpy, dour, and a few of the other lesser-known Disney dwarfs.

We met in his office, which sat at the diagonally opposite corner of the building to mine.

I said, "You heard about FPP?"

"Of course."

Ron had worked within Wyx-Fin's software development department forever, and he still rolled up his sleeves and got his hands dirty whenever we had any particularly ugly technical problems. He was a very well-informed, highly respected part of the Wyx-Fin furniture who knew more of what was going on than I did.

He pulled out his large, battered ring-binder from his desk's top drawer and sighed. "You need me to free up space in January and early February for CORETRAN bug fixing?"

"I do. And maybe November and December too."

He grimaced, opened his binder and flipped through few pages. He plucked out a thick section and placed it on his desk. Each page represented a single request to change the CORETRAN system.

He pointed to the stack. "That's all the list #1 CORETRAN work we've got lined up between now and the end of the year."

I nodded. Each of Ron's teams operated with his three-list system. List #1 was a long list of requests not yet started. List #2 held the requests currently being worked on; it was a thin list. And List #3 was an ever-growing list of finished requests. He'd worked this way since Ada Lovelace was a programmer, and although it was simplistic, he refused to adopt anything more sophisticated—let alone digitized.

I looked at the first page, read its summary description, then flipped through a few more pages. "Which of these requests can we afford to bump to next year, if we have to?"

"Seventeen are mandatory, and there'll be some serious chest thumping if we don't do another thirty or forty of them. The rest ... well, I've haven't promised when—or if—we'll deliver, so I can bump them to later next year and free up some space with no harm.

I nodded. "We'll probably have to do that. Shall I smooth the waters with the business?"

"No," he gruffed. "They're my customers. They understand the nature of CORETRAN work. They'll happily take what they can get, because none of them want to get on my bad side."

Ron was a grumpy old fella, I thought, but he was also flexible in a crisis.

Soon after leaving Ron, I met with Declan McGuiness, our local employee rep and also one of my developers, and laid out our plans. It was a courtesy call. I wasn't looking for his input or his permission.

Gregor and I met with Eleanor, Mark Richmond and Catherine in Eleanor's office after lunch to confirm our rescue plan.

Gregor spoke with confidence, and they seemed relieved.

Mark offered his profound thanks and said he'd buy Gregor and me a pint sometime.

Even Eleanor, who is naturally less generous with her praise, thanked me for my good work as she ushered Gregor, Catherine and me out of her office.

All in all, it was a good day. We were back on track.

For now.

Tuesday, August 8th
FPP launch date - February 1st, next year

CHAPTER THIRTEEN

I met Craig Lally on Tuesday morning, at 9:55, in the staff cafeteria as promised. I'd cleared my schedule until noon, and then I would head to the airport for my flight to Copenhagen. As I walked downstairs, FPP's requirements folder gripped firmly under my arm, I reminded myself that I only had to stay with Craig for long enough to appear open-minded when I described our meeting to Norbert in Malmö later that week.

I recognized him from his company photo. He sat at a table at the back, near the corporate gym. A small notebook sat in front of him on the table. He was tieless and wore a functional grey suit, and appeared to be late-50s. He looked like a man who'd climbed a lot of mountains in his time—for pleasure—and drove to the mountains in a twenty-year-old Volvo he maintained himself.

He stood when I approached him, smiling broadly, and held out his hand. We shook, and I laid FPP's requirements binder on the table. Then we went to the cafeteria counter to grab brunch. We returned a few minutes later, me with fruit and yogurt, a single slice of bacon and coffee, him with bacon and eggs and green tea.

He took a sip of his tea and nodded. "How long have you worked for the Wyxcomb Group, Steve?"

As I took the lid off my coffee to let it cool, I explained that I'd joined nineteen years earlier as a graduate programmer. I'd worked in different roles, rising through the company, until my most recent promotion as development manager. During my time with Wyx-

Group, I'd lived for a few years in Sweden and Canada, until Fran and I had returned to live in Watt's Bridge with our family. From there I had commuted to Glasgow to one of Wyxcomb Bank's development centers, doing a job similar to the one I did now.

I didn't share this bit with Craig, but my Watt's Bridge job was a smaller, easier job than the Glasgow role, and under normal circumstances my position would be viewed as a demotion. When I returned to work following Fran's death, my predecessor at Wyx-Fin and I swapped jobs. She got a promotion and a considerably longer commute, and I got a less challenging job closer to my home and my kids. Since then, though the job had grown with FPP, and over time I'd deliberately taken on more work for Norbert. Which is why I traveled a lot now.

"I'd heard that promotion within Wyxcomb's IT departments was on a dead men's shoes basis. Have you had many bosses die under suspicious circumstances, or are you good at your job?"

"A little bit of both," I laughed. "I caught a lucky break early on in my career, and the luck seems to follow me.

"Norbert said your team, overall, consists of about one hundred fifty staff."

I nodded, and then shared a few facts and figures. I actually had nearer two hundred staff, if you included the two dozen contractors we'd brought on to deliver FPP. Most of them worked full-time on FPP, while the rest either worked on smaller projects or beavered away in Ron McKnight's Support and Maintenance team churning out hundreds of smaller fixes and enhancements each year. The remaining few worked in management and administrative roles, including my small project management office.

"How long have you been in this job?"

"Just over two years."

"So you've managed FPP's development from the start?"

"Yes."

Craig said, "Okay. Good. Let's get started."

He opened the notebook to a blank page.

"There's one tool—a simple diagram—I need to show you. It's a thinking tool. I can teach it to you in just a few minutes. It will help us both to understand your problems, and later it will help us generate solutions."

"Okay."

He cleared his throat. "Whenever I want to solve a significant problem, I describe it using this diagram called an evaporating cloud." He saw me lift a cynical eyebrow, and he raised his hand in response. "I know it sounds odd, but trust me, it's the most useful tool I've ever used."

He pulled an expensive-looking pen from his pocket and sketched a small stick person, with an unhappy face, in the middle of the blank page.

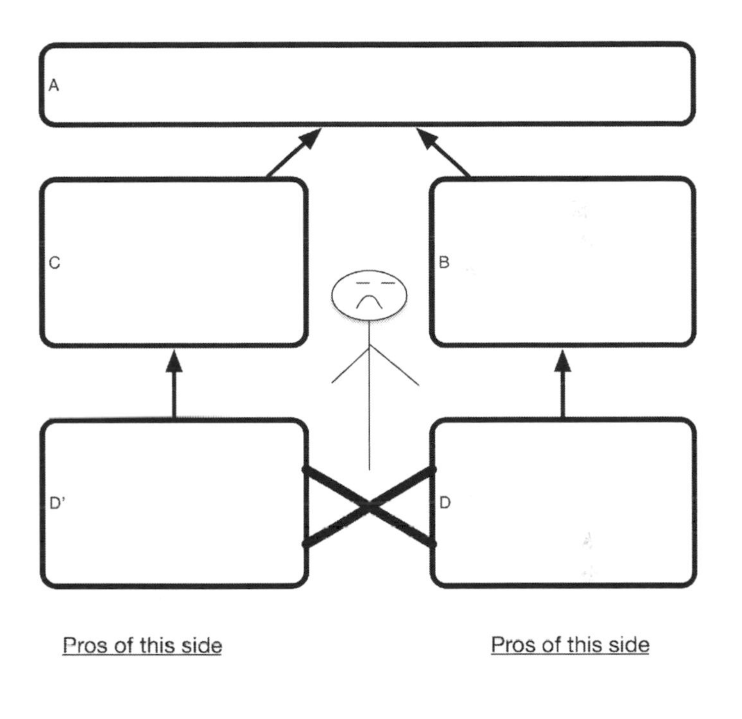

He added five big rectangles, one pair below the man's hands, one pair sitting above the stickman's shoulders, and one hovering over its head. He labeled the boxes, *A, B, C, D,* and *D'*. He drew arrows between the boxes then scribbled some text at the bottom of the page.

Craig turned the pad to face me, then started by holding his hands out in front of him. "The hand boxes represent conflicting options or choices." He curled his left hand into a fist. "On the one hand ..." He clenched his right hand. "But on the other hand ..."

He tapped his shoulders. "Each shoulder represents the weights we carry on our shoulders. The concerns or needs—the things that are threatened or jeopardized by choosing one option over the other."

Then, with both hands palms open, he circled around his head and upper body and said, "The top box represents your highest level needs and goals: the needs of the head, the heart, or the gut."

"Okay," I said, looking doubtful.

"Let's use the work I did with Wyxcomb Health as an example. We'll start with D and D-prime—the two hands, the two conflicting choices. In Wyx-Health's case, it was simply a conflict between buying or building a new system."

He wrote *Build* in the left box D', the one he called D-prime, and *Buy* in the right-hand D box.

"On the one hand they could build, on the other hand they could buy. With me?"

"So far, yes."

"Good. Let's move up a level to the C box. We need to find a short sentence which sums up the reasons why we want to *Build*. What concerns does *building* address?" He tapped the C box with his pen. "We find that sentence by listing out two things: first, the positives we get from building, and second, the negatives we avoid by not buying. Does that make sense?"

It took me a moment to figure out what *the negatives we avoid by not buying* meant. I said, "I think so."

"When we spoke, you pointed out several benefits of having Wyx-Health software build the replacement. Do you remember them?"

I didn't recall our conversation verbatim, but it was easy enough to list three reasons off the top of my head. He scribbled these under the D-prime box.

Pros for building in-house

(1) Our development staffs' hourly rates are lower than the vendors'

(2) We can customize the product how and when we want

(3) Our existing staff keep their jobs

He said, "Good. Now tell me, can you think of any cons of doing the opposite? Buying?"

I listed five cons out loud. Three were direct opposites of the pros I'd already listed and Craig said we could ignore them. He scribbled down the two distinct cons.

Cons for buying

(4) Future work might get delayed while the vendor works on our competitors' requests

(5) The vendor might overcharge us when doing our change requests because we can't easily switch—we become "hostages"

Craig took a sip from his green tea and said, "These three pros and two cons are the reasons we might choose to build. Can you take a shot at summarizing them all into one concise sentence?"

"Is that what goes in the C box?"

He nodded.

I read the five points over again twice before I ventured forward with a summary. "If we build, then we have more control over development."

"The Wyx-Health folk said something similar," he said, and wrote *More control over development* in the C box.

"Let's move to the B box." He tapped the tip of his pen on the B box. "This box is often harder to fill out. In fact, the Wyx-Health development team was so firmly in favor of building they couldn't think of *any* benefits of buying until they got in the same room as their business guys."

I nodded as I recalled my own reaction to our earlier phone conversation. "You said the Wyx-Health business wanted to get to market quickly, to start selling again, to start making money."

"Correct. That was the significant benefit of buying." He nodded and wrote *Pro- Start selling far sooner* under the right-hand side of the little stick

man. "There was also one significant con of building that drove the business guys to favor buying." He frowned, which I thought was ominous. "Can you think of it?"

I couldn't.

He grimaced as he spoke. "The Wyx-Health business had no faith in their technology team's ability to build a replacement."

I felt my shoulders rise, but I said nothing.

He sensed my reaction and leaned in towards me. "Don't get me wrong. They trusted the team's motives, just not their competence. It was a big project."

My shoulders relaxed as I realized he was right. That team had spent years keeping an old, broken system alive, so they were unlikely to have the managerial or technical experience to build a mission-critical, brand new system. I said, "That's fair. It would take them a long time to build a replacement, and it would be risky."

He wrote: *Con- In-house development riskier and slower.*

"Let me show you what they put in their B box." He wrote: *Pull in Revenue ASAP*. "With me?"

"Yes."

"Note that D and D' conflict but B and C do not."

Then he wrote *Profitable Business* in the A box over the stick figure's head, the one labeled *Common Goal.*

He said, "It's important when drawing your clouds to hunt for the mutual purpose, or common goal, that joins both sides together."

"What if there isn't a common goal?"

He frowned, as if he'd never seen that situation before. "Keep looking, I guess."

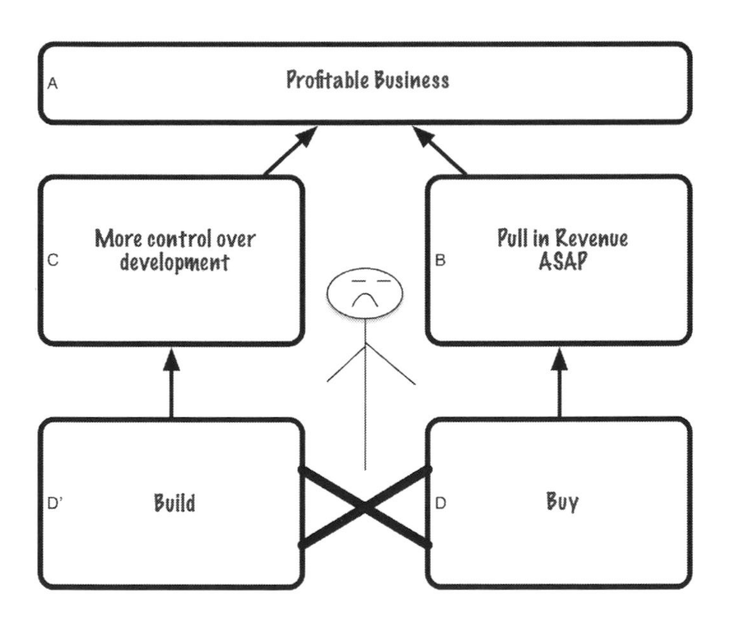

He carefully tore the page from his notepad and handed it to me. "There are several ways to evaporate clouds, but let's work through the pros and cons listed here to see how Wyx-Health evaporated this cloud. First, it's important to recognize that A, B and C are most important. D and D' are just alternative means to more important ends."

I said, "In order to achieve their goal of having a profitable business, they needed to do two things: bring in more revenue ASAP and also retain control of their future development work."

"Correct," he said. "Now, you know the way this thing went. Wyx-Health bought a replacement system, but they also worked with the new vendor to create a win-win contract. By choosing to buy, they achieved the pros of buying and avoided the negatives of building. By negotiating a win-win contract they, hopefully, incentivized the vendor in a way that avoided the two cons of buying. I say 'hopefully' because you can never be sure about these things."

I nodded and mentally ticked off items #4 and #5 on the left.

"But that still left the three pros of building. Let's work backwards. They addressed #3 by getting the existing staff to work first on the new system, and then in time migrate from the old to the new system. The staff is, apparently, happy with that arrangement. The Wyx-Health business said they didn't want to customize their product, so #2 was a reasonable concern but an invalid assumption. And, since the development costs were trivial compared to the potential revenue gains, everyone agreed that #1 was a red herring. Make sense?"

I took my time and studied the diagram, then nodded. "So, to sum up: You drew the cloud, you picked a side, then you figured out how to make the bad bits from the other side irrelevant?"

"That makes it seem easy! We actually spent hours thrashing this out. And, we didn't just pick one side. The team looked seriously at both sides before choosing to buy. They also considered ways they could achieve B and C without building or buying. It was fun, for me, but it certainly wasn't easy. We had some hard conversations."

"I imagine."

He leaned forward and placed his pen on the table in front of me. "Now, it's your turn."

CHAPTER FOURTEEN

I picked up Craig's pen and reluctantly reached across and pulled the pad close to me. "What problem do you want me to tackle?"

He said, "Norbert told me about your FPP situation. How about if we start with that?"

I glanced at the Wyx-Health cloud and copied the stickman shape, the boxes and the arrows. "That was the easy bit. What next?"

He said step one was to tell him off the top of my head, as quickly as I could, what the problem was.

I nodded. "I don't know for sure if I can deliver FPP on February 1st."

"Why not write that at the top of the page."

I looked at his pen. It felt good and solid, well-balanced in my hand. I concentrated as I wrote, taking extra care to write tidily.

Craig told me that step two was to fill out the D box by answering the question *What action do I find myself complaining about?*

I played his question back silently in my head. It seemed easy enough.

But it wasn't. I couldn't quite think what to write. I hesitated, and then confessed I wasn't sure.

He smiled gently. "Are you, maybe, just a little nervous about getting it wrong?"

"No. Well, yeah. A little bit."

"You don't have to get it right the first time. Paper and ink are cheap. Just tell me: What's pissing you off?"

I bit down on the inside of my lip. I thought of all the things that bothered me, and then decided the ONE thing that really pissed me off was that we'd already used our industry's only secret weapon: poor quality. We were deliberately shipping a crappy product, loaded with defects and barely fit for purpose. It sickened me, but I felt I had no option.

I explained this to Craig, and together we hashed it. I wrote *Shipping a poor quality, inadequately featured product on February 1st* in the D box.

He nodded. "Our third step is to fill in the D-prime box by answering this question: *What is your desired, opposite action of D?*"

With more enthusiasm this time, I wrote: *Shipping a product that is good quality and with adequate features.*

He lifted his hands and weighed the two options, as if he were comparing the weight of two melons. "So, on the one hand, you ship good stuff. On the other hand, you ship not so good stuff."

He put his hands down and asked me to fill out the C box by answering *What need is satisfied by the action in D-prime?*

I said, "Is this when I list the pros of D-prime and the cons of D, like we did with the buy/build cloud, then use them to figure out what goes in C?"

"You've got it now."

So I listed off the benefits of shipping quality and then the negatives of shipping poor quality. It wasn't difficult. Customers would like our product, presumably buy more of it, maybe even tell their friends about it. We'd make more sales. Our staff would be proud. The cost to support it, after it went live, would be far lower. We could use our staff on other projects, rather than bug-fixing. We wouldn't face any big risks—reputational or more concrete. I could have gone on, but I didn't need to.

So what summed them up? Quality was quality was quality. How could I say it in a sentence? I asked Craig to describe the C box again.

"Figuring out B and C can sometimes be tricky. If you're stuck, then try asking this question instead: *What is jeopardized by doing D?*"

I sighed. What did that even mean?

He said, "Imagine using the index finger on your D hand to jab yourself firmly in the opposite shoulder, C. That finger would hurt your shoulder. Doing D hurts or jeopardizes something. What is it?"

I looked at the D box. What did shipping crap jeopardize?

"Shipping crap jeopardizes the product's commercial viability. We might keep Hal happy short-term, but we won't sell anything and we will damage our long-term credibility."

Craig smiled and said, "Can you shorten that a bit?"

I thought a moment, then wrote *Delivering a product that sells well for a long time and makes us proud* in the C box.

We moved to step five, completing the B box. Craig reminded me that we started with box D, something we didn't like but we did anyway. Why was that? What did I get out of doing D? Why did I put up with D?

What were the pros of shipping a poor quality product? We were more likely to deliver on time and budget. We'd beat Chaste to Market. Hal would keep whatever promise he'd made to the Group. I'd keep my job. And the cons of taking longer and delivering a proper product? There was only one I could think of: FPP could take a very long time to meet the market. I wrote *Deliver FPP according to Hal's schedule* in the B box.

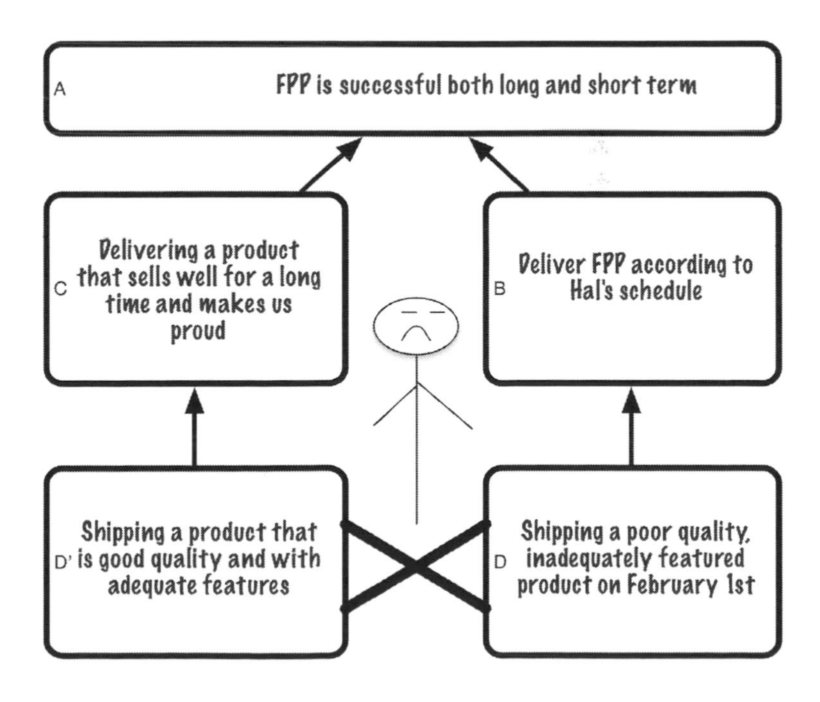

For the last step, we filled in the A box with: *FPP is successful both long and short term.* That seemed obvious at the time, but as I would discover much later, it did not tell the full story. If only I'd known then what was really going on in Hal's world.

We then tweaked the wording of the cloud. Craig said, "Read it out loud. Start from the top and work down, like this: *In order to, A we must B* and *In order to A, we must C* and so on."

I did as I was told.

He said, "Now check that D and D-prime actually do conflict with each other."

I verified they were indeed opposites, that I couldn't do both at the same time.

"Two final sanity checks," he said. "Does doing D really jeopardize C? And does doing D-prime really jeopardize B?"

I checked, then said they did.

"Good." He reached across and ripped the page out. He handed the pad back to me and asked me to write the cloud out fresh, from memory.

I did, changing the language a little more. It took about a minute, and afterward I felt surprisingly calm.

I saw the enemy. It wasn't Chaste. It wasn't Hal or Eleanor, and it wasn't the Group.

"We can't win as long as this cloud exists."

Craig nodded solemnly. "That's why we draw it."

CHAPTER FIFTEEN

And then something strange happened.

Feeling rather pleased, I picked up the pad and read the cloud back to myself again. Then I read it again, and then again—and then again. Each reading it became more familiar. And the more familiar it became, the less exciting it seemed. In less than two minutes, my diagram transformed from something fresh and enlightening into something familiar and old. I realized that I'd known it all along, and I found myself annoyed that I'd just spent precious time drawing a picture of something I already knew.

I glanced at my watch, but it was too soon to leave without appearing disrespectful to Craig—and to Norbert.

I pointed at the paper. "Isn't all this obvious?"

"Is it? Good. That probably means it's correct."

I frowned at his answer.

He leaned forward. "It's a specific example of a very common conflict, Steve."

"What do you mean?"

"Do you think you're the first project, or business, or even industry to think you can go faster by sacrificing quality?"

I shrugged. "Probably not."

"For some reason, most people view them as alternatives; you either get quality or speed, not both. But if I were to sum up the entire quality movement in a short sentence, it is this: Quality, done right, increases speed and productivity."

I smiled. "That's your thing—quality—so you would say that."

He didn't smile back. "Quality is just one of my three main things: Quality, Lean Thinking and the Theory of Constraints."

He leaned back in his chair. I waited for him to draw me a picture of a three-legged stool or a pyramid, but he didn't. He just sat back and smiled.

The ball was in my court. "Do you really think I can solve this problem with FPP?"

He shifted, just a little, in his seat. "I don't, actually. I suspect the die is cast for FPP—you've been working on it for many months now, after all. All you can do is wait and see what numbers come up. What we *can* do with FPP is use it to prevent the next FPP."

I looked down at the pad then back up to him again. I was dubious, but at least he hadn't tried to outsource my team.

I said, "What's next?"

"I want to show you a living example of how Lean and Quality Thinking dramatically improved the lives of hundreds of people in this building. I suspect you have the same problems, and maybe you can use the same principles—though not the same practices—to evaporate your cloud."

I frowned and said, "Why not just skip to the last page and tell me who did the murder?"

"You won't believe me if I tell you. You'd just argue with me. You need to hear the story, and then figure out which bits apply to you. Trust me, Steve. This is how I work."

"Okay," I said tentatively. "Tell me then, which business is your showcase?"

"Before I tell you, you must promise to spend at least the next hour with me."

"Promise? I'm not five years old, you know."

He raised his eyebrows but remained silent.

"Okay." I threw my hands in the air to make light of my exasperation. "I promise."

"You're sitting in it."

I looked around. "The cafeteria?"

He smiled and shrugged the world's tiniest shrug.

"You're serious?"

He nodded the world's smallest nod.

I considered refusing, but I decided to give him ten minutes. Then, if it wasn't working out, I'd break my promise and walk away. Norbert would understand. Some promises aren't worth keeping.

Craig stood and started walking towards the cafeteria's serving area. I rushed to catch up with him. I noticed that he walked with a limp.

He spoke quietly as I fell in place beside him. "I joined the TCQ team three years ago, after Group offshored my factory to Indonesia. It was that or early retirement. My wife threatened to leave me for a younger man if I took early retirement, so here I am.

"My new TCQ colleagues worried that my manufacturing skills would not be very useful in offices and call centers, so they started me out on something safe—a test, I suppose—helping facilities outsource the running of this cafeteria."

He slowed and turned to catch my eye. "And guess what?"

"What?"

"My manufacturing skills *were* helpful, and they've been helpful in every assignment since. And guess what else."

"What?"

He didn't answer right away, and we continued ahead to the service area, where he stopped me with a light hand on my shoulder. "In the end we didn't outsource anyone."

He gestured for me to step through the gap between the salad bar and the cash registers, moving from the public part of the cafeteria into the working part. I felt like I was trespassing, but I did as I was told.

CHAPTER SIXTEEN

Craig waved to one of the servers. "How you doing, Randall?" he said.

Randall, a burly guy wearing the cafeteria staff's ninja-style black uniform and a black chef's hat, sliced through the strings on a roasted beef joint with a large carving knife.

"Aye, I'm grand, Craig. Thank you for asking. Cheryl is in the kitchen. She's expecting you."

Craig led me into the kitchen, then waved at a thin, short, middle-aged woman carrying a clipboard and pacing while talking on a portable phone. I guessed she was Cheryl.

Spotting Craig, she smiled broadly and mouthed *two minutes*. She waved us towards a small office. I listened as we passed her. It sounded like she was making the following day's vegetable order.

While we sat waiting in the office, Craig said, "Like I said, my new TCQ boss wanted me to help outsource the cafeteria operations. But since many of my friends had just lost their jobs offshore, I didn't like that idea. Instead, I helped the cafeteria team turn around their operation so that it no longer made sense to outsource them. It was easy for me—the kitchen is just a small factory—but not so easy for them."

He paused to let that last sentence sink in.

"The cafeteria suffered two classic manufacturing problems: a flow problem, which the cafeteria staff named their French Fry Revelation, and a quality problem they call their Dog Food Problem. Both were interrelated."

"Strange names."

"Sometimes it helps to name new concepts, especially if you pick a sticky name. The concepts are straightforward. Cheryl will explain."

Cheryl arrived and Craig stood up to greet her. They hugged, then Cheryl turned to me and stuck out her hand. "I'm Cheryl. I manage this place. You must be Steve."

I said, "I am," and we shook hands. She had a strong grip for such a tiny lady.

"Craig says you're one of those clever computer whiz kids from upstairs."

I nodded.

"And that you've got yourself in a bit of a mess and you need old Cheryl to show you how to sort it out?"

I felt my face redden, but I nodded. "Something like that."

"Good. First, can you take off your tie, please?"

"Of course." I imagined my tie being sucked into a pasta machine, turning it and then me into tagliatelle. "Is it a safety hazard?"

"No, it's because you look like a dork."

She said it in such a nice way that I did as I was told. I even smiled a little.

Cheryl led me on a quick tour of the kitchen, starting at the back door where the fresh ingredients were dropped each morning. We popped into a walk-in chiller then quickly back out again (it was cold). She pointed out the various jobs her team was performing as they prepared for the upcoming lunchtime rush. I saw a lot of chopping, stirring and cleaning. I smelled a bundle of pleasing odors, the sweet-savory smell of onions frying dominating. She trotted to the swinging doors that separated the kitchen from the serving area and pushed one open. "We serve hundreds, sometimes thousands, of meals each day. I've seen you in the queue, Steve, so you know how it works."

I said I did and that I recognized her, too. She seemed happy about that.

Cheryl turned to Craig. "Shall I tell Steve about our miracle turnaround, then?"

Craig tilted his head from side to side, as if wondering if that was a good idea, then nodded emphatically, as if he'd just made a profoundly important decision. "Why not?"

I glanced at my watch. My self-imposed ten minute limit was almost up, but I decided to hang around a little longer. It couldn't hurt, and I didn't want to seem impolite to Cheryl. She seemed like a nice lady. And she prepared most of my lunches.

"Come through here," Cheryl said as she led us out through the swinging doors to stand beside the serving area. Randall had gone, leaving the roasted beef and a pork roast, complete with gravy, resting under the heating lamps for the call center staff whose shifts forced them to take their lunch earlier than most.

She asked me how long I'd been working at Wyx-Fin. I told her I'd spent nineteen years within the Wyxcomb Group. She called me a newbie. She'd worked in the canteen for twenty-eight years.

"So," she said, "up until about three years ago our food was barely fit for human consumption. You wouldn't feed it to a dog. Well, not a posh dog; a stray would eat it if there were no alternatives. We called this our Dog Food problem.

"Our bosses said our food cost too much and that our customers hated it. They wanted to lay us off and replace us with a commercial catering operation. They were right about the problem, wrong about the cure."

She pointed to Craig. "That's when Craig turned up and forced us to eat our own dog food."

Craig smiled, managing to look both proud and modest at the same time.

"He spent two weeks with us, and with only one change in staff and no changes in our food suppliers, we were soon cooking food our customers liked. Now, as I'm sure you know, nothing travels faster than word of good quality, affordable food within walking distance. After a month, we were serving nearly twice as many customers as before, our average costs dropped way down, and the threat to replace us disappeared.

"Would you like to hear how that happened?"

I said I would. It was hard to say otherwise.

CHAPTER SEVENTEEN

Cheryl glanced sideways at Craig. "Craig booked lunch with my old boss and me here in the canteen and told us our food tasted horrible," She turned to Craig. "You can be awfully blunt sometimes, can't you?"

He smiled and she continued with her story. "My boss, a big opinionated lady from Dundee, told Craig to go screw himself. She didn't come in the next day, and I was offered to take on her job."

"On one condition," smiled Craig. "One horrifying condition."

Cheryl sighed, as if the memory of the horror was still fresh with her. "Craig insisted we ate the same food we served our customers. If we did, he said, he'd give us permission to change how we worked and improve the food, so that we all got to keep our jobs and Wyxcomb pensions. And eventually we could even have nice lunches every day."

"Why on earth would Craig have to give you *permission* to improve?"

Craig said, "Over the years, the cafeteria staffs' jobs had been dumbed-down and standardized to the point where they were meant to be idiot-proof."

"Idiot-proof!" Cheryl spat the words out like they were poison. "Our bosses thought we were idiots because we didn't wear suits to work. But what we achieved here since then, after we started breaking their idiot-proof rules, proved them wrong."

I glanced at Craig. He was nodding enthusiastically. I, on the other hand, was struggling to see how this was relevant to me.

"Could you show me some of your improvements?"

Cheryl nodded, then led us to a couple of soup-warmer pots. One was labeled Tomato Soup, the other Thai Chicken Noodle Soup.

"These are called soup kettles. Soup is cheap, easy to cook and hard to screw up. If the stock and the other ingredients are good, then the soup's good. But, crazy as this sounds, our soup often tasted horrible. You want to know why?"

"Of course."

"No one ever tasted it before serving it."

"Pardon?"

"No one ever tasted it before serving it."

"No way."

"Yes way, Steve. We cooked food, from scratch, following supposedly 'foolproof' recipes and menus provided to us by Head Office. We followed the recipes to the letter, but no one tested them to see how they tasted!"

She stopped talking again and stared at me. I realized I was supposed to ask her why no one ever tasted the soup. I obliged.

"Why not?"

"Well, I'm embarrassed to admit it now, but—frankly—we didn't care." She shrugged her shoulders with indifference. "We sold basic food, which we cooked by following basic, foolproof recipes. It's not like we were professional chefs chosen for our cooking skills; we were chosen for our ability to follow simple instructions and not ask too many questions. None of us ate the food we sold and none of us particularly cared about the food we sold. We worked our hours, what more could you ask from us?"

I looked around the kitchen, and everyone seemed to be engaged and working hard. I couldn't match what she was describing with what I saw.

"What changed?"

"By threatening to outsource our jobs, our bosses gave us a reason to worry and to change. By insisting we eat our own food, Craig gave us a reason to care about our product."

I nodded.

"Can you guess what the first change was?"

That wasn't hard. "Did you start tasting your food before you served it?"

She smiled and nodded. "Yup. And often we fixed things with a little salt or some pepper. Sometimes it was a little trickier. If we couldn't fix it, we threw away the food."

I flinched. "Ouch. Wasn't that expensive?"

Craig said, "Not as expensive as having not enough customers."

"And that was just the first stopgap step." She looked at Craig. "You had a name for what we did next, but I can never remember what it is."

He said, "You moved from late inspections—testing or tasting at the end of the process when it's very expensive to fix stuff—to in-process inspections, where you build quality into your product during the process."

Cheryl nodded emphatically. "Okay, Steve. Here's what in-process inspections meant for us when cooking soup. It meant we checked the ingredients were up to standards before using them. So we'd taste the stock before we put it into the soup kettle. You don't want to use bad stock, cook the soup in it for hours, and then taste it and throw it out."

I nodded. That was just common sense. "And, I guess, you'd check the meat and vegetables were up to standards too, before you put them in. That's what I'd do if I was cooking soup at home."

"Of course you would. You'd check the raw ingredients were good. You'd taste and smell things. You'd test them to see if they're cooked."

"Right."

"At first we worried all that extra testing and tasting would take us a lot of time, time we didn't have. But it didn't and it still doesn't."

Craig added, "Especially when the alternative was tossing product then cooking a new batch of soup from scratch."

She folded her arms in front of her. "Within two weeks, we'd transformed the quality of our food. And that was the first time I truly enjoyed working here." She pointed to some of her team on the other side of the room, putting fresh flowers on the dining tables. "I wasn't the only one."

I glanced at my watch again, then pulled my phone from my pocket and checked its screen. I had twenty-one new emails and three missed calls. I forced a smile and said to Cheryl: "That's a nice story." I meant it, but I guess maybe I didn't sound like I meant it enough.

Cheryl's smile dropped into a deep frown. "It's more than nice. It's a bloody miracle. They were going to shut us down, but with a few tweaks over a few weeks, Craig saved our jobs"

She looked at Craig, frowned, and said rather bluntly. "Looks like we've got another skeptic here."

He smiled gently. "Steve and I are still in the early stages of our discussions."

I didn't like the way they'd suddenly taken to speaking about me as if I wasn't there. I took a small step back. "You know," I said defensively, "my staff already does extensive in-process inspections throughout our entire development process."

Cheryl said, "Oh?"

"We inspect our requirements documents, our design documents and our specification documents. And, we have very strict code inspection and walkthrough processes. We're a big company, we have big processes mandated on us from HQ, and we follow them to the letter. We don't cut corners."

Craig said, "These inspections, are they like looking at the soup or like tasting it?"

"Looking or tasting? What do you mean?"

"Are you inspecting—*looking*— at words and code, or are you testing—*tasting*—that the software actually acts as you expect? The former is inspection, the latter is testing."

"Both. We do a lot of inspection, and our developers also extensively test the software they write as they build it. They even automate some of that testing."

"Wyx-Health didn't mention any of those things."

"I wouldn't expect them to. Given how you described them, they weren't doing big projects like us, they were making small fixes and enhancements to an old legacy system."

Suddenly he didn't look as confident as he had a few minutes earlier. "So you inspect and test during your development phase, but then, despite that, you still require a long testing phase afterwards?"

I nodded.

Cheryl surprised me by asking the next question. "How long does your testing phase last, Steve?"

I frowned. "It depends. On medium to large projects we'd typically spend thirty percent, or more, of each project in the testing phase."

"And during that phase you are both testing and reworking?"

I nodded.

Cheryl then let out a long whistle. "No way. Really? You spend thirty percent of your time fixing broken stuff?"

I glared at her, deciding then that I didn't like her, and that I'd spent enough time in her kitchen. I turned to Craig and blocked her from my view. "Can we speak in private?"

He frowned, realizing, I guess, that he'd lost me. "I suppose."

I turned back to Cheryl. "Thank you for your time, Cheryl." I smiled, and I meant it. "And thank you not just for now, but for saving the cafeteria. The food, the service, they're much better now than they were. Much better. And now I know why."

She smiled and thanked me, then dropped the smile and said sternly, "You do realize that you haven't heard the full story yet? You need to hear about our French Fry Revelation before it fully makes sense."

"I don't have time," I said softly.

She made a face, as if she'd smelled something bad. "We'll see," she said, and then walked off without saying goodbye.

Craig sighed. "Let's go talk."

CHAPTER EIGHTEEN

We walked back to the coffee area without speaking. I picked up my folder of requirements from the table. I didn't sit.

I said, "I'm sorry Craig. I know you know your stuff, but I don't have time for this now."

"I understand your reluctance but you should know this: Given what I've heard about how you work, I know I can help you."

I was dubious. "Really? You can help me deliver FPP on Hal's arbitrary date without sacrificing too much quality?"

"No, but I can help you figure out how to prevent the next FPP debacle. I'm sure of it."

I took in a deep breath and looked him directly in the eyes. I knew he was serious. But with FPP, which was the only thing I really cared about right then, he was too late. I think we both knew that.

"I do not need your help, Craig."

He flinched, and for a moment I regretted my words.

"Look. You just can't compare a kitchen with a software development organization. We are just too different."

Craig's face lit up. "Tell me more about that."

I shook my head. "I don't have time."

"Two minutes is all it will take. Tell me why they're different."

"Okay. But If I tell you, will you tell Norbert we played together nicely?"

His smile faltered. "If that's what matters to you, yes."

Good. I had what I wanted.

I said, "I don't think you, with your manufacturing background, can possibly appreciate the scale of what we do. Our software is enormously more complex and complicated than any physical product manufactured anywhere in the world."

He pulled a face, clearly unconvinced.

"How many components do you think a large airliner has?" I said, though I had no idea what the answer was.

He shrugged, "A few million, I guess."

"And how many customers does it carry at one time?"

"A few hundred."

"My team upstairs looks after forty-seven million lines of code. And that's only what we've written ourselves over the decades; if you included the off-the-shelf components we use, that number would be five, ten times bigger. Maybe more. The software we build manages millions of transactions worth many millions each week, for over six million customers.

"Print out an aircraft's schematic designs then weigh them. I'll do the same with my code base. I think we both know which would be heavier."

"You're right, but I don't think you can compare the two like that."

"And I don't think you should compare my software development project with a kitchen."

He nodded, then said, "We seem to be arguing."

"We do."

"Let's find something we can agree on, then." He pointed towards the cafeteria's kitchen. "Those guys cook their food using a very different workflow than the people who created the recipes in the first place. Do you agree?"

"Of course. Developing a new recipe would be iterative and would require a lot of trial and error. Cooking a recipe should be foolproof." Then, recalling the conversation we had just had, I added, "Or, at least, foolproof subject to the quality of the ingredients and sensible processes."

"So which of the two processes—developing the recipe or cooking it— does your software development process resemble most?"

That was easy. "The development process, of course. We are called software *development*, after all. We develop the recipes—the algorithms, the step-by-step instructions—which our computers execute, or if you like, cook."

"Interesting." He tilted his head to one side and smiled. "To me, speaking as an outsider, your industry's core problem seems to be that you build software based on a model that is applicable to manufacturing, or cooking, but you don't do manufacturing. You do development. We should discuss that."

He gestured towards the seat, inviting me to sit.

I kept my face neutral. I saw what he was doing. He was trying to create a gap in my head which I could only fill if I stayed and talked. But I was too wily to fall for that old trick. Instead, I leaned forward and we shook. "Another time, maybe."

"Maybe. Maybe not." He shrugged again then smiled, as if to show he held no grudge. "I'll email Norbert and let him know we had a useful conversation, but that we're not taking it any further."

He stood, and I watched him walk over to Cheryl who was talking with some of her staff by the cash registers.

Wednesday, August 16th
FPP launch date - February 1st, next year

CHAPTER NINETEEN

Life rolled along fine for the next week or so, until precisely 2:22 p.m. the following Wednesday when the shit hit the fan.

I should have worn goggles to work that day.

I was in our weekly project status meeting with two exchange staff who were nearing the end of a six-month stint in Watt's Bridge and would soon be returning to their home office in Madrid. We were just about to wrap up when someone rapped on my office door.

I opened it. It was Eleanor.

"Where the hell is your staff? How the hell will FPP come in on time if no one is working on it?"

"Pardon?"

She looked past me, noticed I had company and then forced on a clearly false smile and politely asked them to leave. I invited her in as they slipped away.

She closed the door. "I just walked past your FPP team space, and apart from a few contractors, the place is deserted."

I said the staff was probably in meetings, that I would check it out and that I really didn't appreciate her interfering. I was sure, I said, that if I happened to be standing outside her office and glanced in, it would be empty. That didn't mean she wasn't working, it just meant she wasn't there.

"One of your contractors snitched. The permanent staff is all on an extended lunch break in a pub. You have a mutiny on your hands."

"I doubt that."

"Listen to me," she said sharply. "Hal is making an announcement this afternoon. It is embargoed until the press release and I can't tell you what it is now, but you should watch your email. It affects you and your team."

I nodded.

"You're not going to like it."

I snorted. "So, he's not resigning then?"

Her mouth opened just a bit, and she forced it shut. "Hal and I are on the next flight to Sweden and I wouldn't have come down here except that I have a message for you from Hal. It's not for anyone else's ears."

I waited.

"Launch FPP on time. Or find a new job."

Bam! I flinched. Boom! It felt like she'd just slammed me across the face with a coal shovel.

She opened my door and stomped out, then slammed the door hard enough to rattle the glass wall.

I winced. Everyone in the office must have heard it.

I sat down and cupped my face in my hands. I waited until I heard the elevator door *ding*, then made my way to the FPP work area. I walked straight-backed, and even though I made no eye contact, I felt the eyes of all my other staff following me as I crossed the building. When I got to the FPP area, I discovered Eleanor was right. The lights were on but none of the permanent FPP staff were home.

No, that's a bad way of putting it. For all I knew, they *were* at home.

I tracked them down by picking on the closest contractor and asking her where everyone had gone. Her reluctance to snitch soon faded when I reminded her I signed off on her agencies' invoices and approved their contract renewals. She suggested I look in a popular lunchtime pub not far from the office.

Eleanor was right. It seemed that Gregor—or more precisely, Gregor and I—had mutiny on our hands.

CHAPTER TWENTY

The pub's official name was The Robbie Burns, after Scotland's great poet, but we locals called it The Burns Unit, since it was right next to Watt's Bridge hospital. It was frequented by hospital staff as well as by people from the nearby offices. There had been much loose talk of renaming it since the smoking ban, but the talk had come to nothing.

It took me five minutes of fast walking to get to the pub. I felt myself get angrier with each footstep. When I got there, I was ready to kick each of their arses a dozen times over.

The pub was dimly lit. Abba's "Dancing Queen" played over the sound system; very traditional. From the looks on their faces when I walked in, I'd guess they were expecting Gregor, not me. Perhaps forty of my staff, almost all of the permies working on the core FPP team, sat in the far corner. Most of them were positioned with a view of the door and all looked like they were drinking freshly-squeezed lemon juice. Big Declan McGuiness, the employee rep, sat among the group. He was frowning, but that wasn't so unusual. My heart sunk when I saw Phil and Vrinda sitting with them as well.

Apart from a few medics spread about the pub, this could have been a Wyx-Fin meeting room.

I caught Vrinda's eye, and she held my gaze in defiance until I conceded by tilting my head towards an empty corner of the pub. She followed my gaze and looked back at Phil, who nodded. We met in the corner next to the dart board. It had three darts sticking out of the bullseye, each at an unnatural angle like someone had pushed them there rather than thrown them.

"What's happening?" I asked, trying to keep my voice steady.

"I tried to warn you, but you ignored me," Vrinda said. She spoke quietly, which I knew meant that she was angry. Unlike most of the crowd, she held a mug of tea.

I glanced at Phil's pint glass. I couldn't judge whether it was half-empty or half-full. With the subtlest of movement from his left eyebrow and the merest hint from his right, he asked me silently if I wanted one. With a barely perceptible tilt of my head, I thanked him but declined with regret.

Vrinda said, "Gregor cancelled everyone's holidays—holidays we'd already rescheduled to suit the project's previous schedule. Then he told a few of us, myself included, to pull up our socks and work more overtime. I already take work home. I have children. He can shove it."

Phil said, "Steve, we're not out to screw you."

"I know that," I said, half wishing I'd accepted his offer of a pint. "But if not me, then who are you trying to screw?"

They said nothing. We all knew Gregor was their bad guy. But didn't they realize that by screwing him, they were screwing me?

Gregor was in a horrible position, and I'd have done exactly the same if I were him. What else could he do?

"You could try giving Gregor a break," I said. "He's had to make some very difficult calls."

I didn't say it, but I couldn't help but think it: A few longer hours every so often in times of crisis wasn't all that much to ask for. Most of the people in this pub had low-rate staff mortgages with Wyx-Fin Bank that were paid straight out of their relatively generous Wyx-Fin salary.

"Look," Phil said, putting his pint glass down on the table and leaning over to pull the darts from the board. "Gregor's made zero friends in the two years since he started working with us. We're all just utterly, utterly sick of working our butts off at the end of every project because your managers can't manage their dates properly."

Phil stepped back from the dart board and took aim. Vrinda and I quickly moved out of his way.

He said, "It's the same pattern in every project: a desperate mad dash at the end that we—and our families—bear the brunt of." He threw his first dart; it hit the board, bounced off, and landed on the floor. As he crouched down to pick it up, he said, "The bottom line is that we are not working impossible hours for the next four months for some futile date."

"Futile? It's not futile, Phil. It's very important that we make this date. Vital."

He turned and gestured at his colleagues on the other side of the room. I looked across at them. Apart from Declan, who raised his pint towards me, they all averted their gaze. I understood; Phil was speaking for everyone.

Phil said, "I didn't say FPP wasn't important, Steve. I said it was futile. Two different concepts. I'll buy you a dictionary for your birthday and you can look them up. Point is, none of us believe we'll make February 1st. And none of us believed we'd make the original date either."

I nodded.

He looked down, breaking eye contact. "I spoke to Ron about it. He more-or-less agreed."

I spun to check the far side of the room. If Ron was among the mutineers then this little get-together wasn't a mutiny, it was a wake, and my best move would be to buy a round of pints and join in the drinking. I scanned the room but, thankfully, Ron wasn't there.

Phil said, "And now Gregor asks us to work compulsory overtime. Time in the office doesn't correlate with productivity. "

"Now, come on a minute," I protested.

"Sure, we get a short burst of productivity, but it soon drops away when we get tired. And then we get sick and tired. And then we just get sick." He cleared his throat. "There's a huge difference between staying late when I feel I can make a difference and working late in order to cover some manager's butt. And that's all this is."

"You think this is a butt-covering exercise?"

He took his time aiming, then threw another dart. It hit the board and stuck this time, just shy of the bullseye.

"If we work our butts off, then how can anyone say that we didn't put our backs into it? How can they blame any of us—especially the PM—when it was obviously an impossible, *futile* date?"

I shook my head. There was that word again. I agreed with everything they said. But that was the game we played.

"What do you want me to do?"

Vrinda answered without hesitation. "One, rescind Gregor's overtime and vacation demands. Two, replace Gregor with someone we respect. Three, let us finish the project properly without artificial pressure."

I bit my lip and looked at my two friends. I needed them on board more than anyone else. But I couldn't replace Gregor even if it might make some people happier in the short term. He wasn't here to make friends, and I had no one else who could do his job.

Then I took a gamble. Unlike Gregor, I *had* made friends. I gestured to an empty booth and asked them to sit down. Phil walked up to the dart board and stuck the remaining dart firmly in the bullseye, then slid in after Vrinda. I sat opposite, then lowered my voice and asked them if they could keep a secret. They both nodded, their faces a mix of curiosity and concern.

"Hal's making an announcement later today and Eleanor wouldn't tell me what it's about."

Phil said, "Well, if you don't know what it's about how can you tell us? That's not a very good secret."

I shook my head. "No, the secret announcement is not the secret I want to tell you. There are two secrets. I need to tell you the second one."

"Are you sure you don't want a pint? You're not making much sense sober."

I ignored him. "Hal just threatened my job."

Vrinda waved that away. "He does that sort of thing all the time. He's all bark and no bite. Everyone knows that."

I shook my head. "No, this time is different. If FPP delivers late then I, apparently, am out on my arse."

She winced. "Ow. That's not a threat, it's an ultimatum."

"Can he do that? Seriously?" Phil asked.

I nodded.

Vrinda's face hardened. "You need us to get back to work?"

I nodded again.

She picked up her mug. "I'll make you a deal, Steve. I'll get this lot back to work, but in return there won't be any compulsory overtime. You can do what you like with Gregor, but if you want to keep your job and deliver on February 1st then we're going to have to slash even more features from the product. And cross our fingers even tighter."

I shook my head. "You honestly think there's more room to de-scope?"

"There is always more room to descope. Always."

I leaned forward. "Okay. I'll talk Gregor down, but you can't tell anyone about Hal's threat."

She stood. "What do you think we are? Stupid?"

Phil slid out of the booth to let Vrinda out, then slid back in as she made her way over to join the rest of the group. I couldn't hear what she said, but within minutes they had downed their drinks, gathered their things and shuffled off to their desks. I watched as they left, but none made eye contact with me. Not even Vrinda.

Phil smirked, "How 'bout we get that pint after all?"

I smiled ruefully and shook my head.

Phil shrugged. "I'll call my mom tonight and ask her to pray for you."

Phil was an atheist, so he got his mom to do his praying for him.

I liked that about him.

CHAPTER TWENTY-ONE

The sunlight blinded me as Phil and I walked out of the gloomy pub. Declan was waiting outside, sucking on what looked like an orange plastic cigar. I presumed it was a nicotine replacement device designed specifically for extraverts.

Spotting us, he asked "You got a minute, Stevie-boy?"

Phil politely excused himself and rushed ahead to join the others. Declan reached inside his jacket pocket, pulled out another plastic cigar—this one lime-green—and offered it to me.

I shook my head, and he pretended to be offended then pretended to stub his cigar out. "I gave up cigarettes and now I'm addicted to these."

We started walking slowly back towards the office.

He said, "That pub's beer is vile."

Declan held very strong opinions about many things, but none more so than beer. He was born and bred in Watt's Bridge. It would be wrong literally to say that Declan was born on the wrong side of the tracks, because in Watt's Bridge the train lines hugged the coast and that would mean he was born at sea. But figuratively it was true. Declan grew up in one of the poorer parts of town with the hard-working have-nots. He studied hard, worked harder and played very little, and nowadays he made a good living working for me as a programmer. He was also my department's unpaid employee rep. The position was meant to be, essentially toothless, but Declan hadn't realized that.

Declan prided himself on speaking plainly. "Your Gregor has righteously messed this one up."

"He's just doing his job."

Declan told me, formally, that formally speaking he wasn't having this conversation and formally speaking he wasn't even in the pub, but that informally he wasn't happy. He hoped to keep things nice and informal. To keep things *within the family.*

I told him that both formally and informally I wasn't happy either. I didn't tell him about Hal's threat. Declan was fair, all things considered, but he was an adversary. Although I respected his intentions, he seemed to think his job was to protect my staff from me and I didn't like that about him.

Neither of us spoke as we walked up St John's Wynd towards the High Street intersection. Watt's Bridge is, according to the tourist books, one of the most pedestrian-friendly cities in Europe, but even the traffic lights were against me that day.

As we waited, I turned to face Declan. "Look Dec, I am taking a long walk with Gregor this afternoon. There will be no forced overtime and vacations are un-cancelled. If you want to lay a formal complaint, well, that's your choice."

I held his stare for a moment. He held mine. He nodded. "We're okay."

The pedestrian lights changed. As we crossed the road, he said, "You look terribly tired, Steve."

I shrugged and said nothing. I felt terribly tired. Too tired to talk about it. My shoulders ached from the weights I carried with me that day.

We walked a short distance up then turned up St Josephine's Close, which was a shortcut to the Wyx-Fin HQ staff entrance. When we reached the entrance, Declan reached into his jacket, pulled out his orange cigar and said, "I'll leave you here then." He pointed towards the smoking shelter. "I need a smoke."

"You know there are no rules against sucking on that thing inside, right?"

He smiled and tipped his head towards the gossiping huddle at the smoking station. "If I did that, how ever would I find out what's really going on in this place?"

He leaned in and spoke confidentially. "If you ever feel like a pint or two one evening, Steve, perhaps a bag of crisps or even a little fish stew," —as far back as Victorian times, folk have traveled up to Watt's bridge to enjoy our famous seaweed bath spas and eat our fish stew—"then I'm in the phone book."

Call his home number. Not his work number. An informal pint.

"Thanks," I said. "Really. Thanks."

We left it at that. He headed towards the smoking shelter, but I had barely swiped my card to go through the revolving door when I heard him shouting. "Steve! Steve!"

I backed away from the door and turned to see Declan rushing towards me.

"The lads just told me that Chaste International just announced they're launching their new product on February 1st," he panted. Good thing he had switched to those orange cigars.

"No way."

"And worse, Hal has just issued a press release announcing that we're launching our product for sale on December 1st."

December 1st. That made no sense. No one would buy the product until April when the new tax year started. And, he'd just robbed me and my team of two months. Why would Hal do that? There was only one reason I could think of.

Hal had just declared war on Chaste.

And I and my team were the collateral damage.

I decided, there and then, to go upstairs and explain to Hal precisely what an arsehole he was.

CHAPTER TWENTY-TWO

I was in a fowl mood when I made it back to my desk. Yes, *fowl*, not foul. While I was in the elevator, somewhere between the second and the fourth floor, the rational part of my brain clicked in. I turned into a big chicken and pushed the button for the sixth floor instead of the penthouse. I'd spent almost twenty years climbing the Wyxcomb ladder, and I wasn't about to throw that all away impulsively.

Instead of giving Hal an excuse to dump me, I summoned Gregor to my office and laid down the law: no compulsory overtime, no cancelled vacations, and start thinking real hard about how to get this project back on track.

His response was a question.

"What would you have done differently?"

"Pardon?"

"If you were in my shoes. What would you have done differently?"

I licked my lips, buying time, then took a deep breath and did the only thing I could. I apologized. He was right. He had done exactly what I would have done had I been in his shoes. And worse, I was doing exactly what my predecessors would have done in my situation. I told him that.

He shrugged and said he was old enough, ugly enough and grumpy enough to be thick-skinned enough to know that sometimes taking the blame was just part of his job.

I shook my head. "But it shouldn't be. We should be better at this."

We left it at that, and I sat down at my desk and tried to figure out what to do next.

I knew I should call Eleanor, but I avoided that conversation and waded through my emails instead. I gave up when I got to one from Hal's personal assistant asking *me* to look at her printer because it was jamming a lot. I shook my head, swore briefly under my breath, then called our help desk manager and asked her to look into it for me.

I called Eleanor.

Her PA answered. Eleanor was mid-flight to Sweden with Hal.

I called Norbert.

He answered immediately and without saying hello: "Can you deliver FPP on December 1st?"

"Realistically?

"Of course, realistically," he said sharply. "We are not playing computer games. You do not have three lives to play with. I ask you again: Will you deliver or not?"

I didn't know what to say.

"Yes or No. Quick."

"No."

"That's what I thought." The phone went silent for a minute. "I don't know if I can help you. If FPP doesn't ship, then Hal is gone. It will be difficult for me to protect you under those circumstances."

He may has well have slapped me across the face. I'd never thought of Norbert as a friend; we were, professionally, closer than that. He was my boss, but also my mentor and protector. After Fran died, it was Norbert who pulled all the bureaucratic strings and corporate levers necessary to transfer me from Glasgow to my current job in Watt's Bridge, nearer my home. Eleanor hadn't wanted me—she wanted someone with smaller ambitions than mine — but he'd insisted. In Wyxcomb, he said, we looked after our own.

His words hurt. He knew the job market in Watt's Bridge for people like me was limited. He knew my family situation and that commuting to either Edinburgh or Glasgow was difficult for me, and that relocating my kids and my mother was damned near out of the question.

I let my breath out. "I need your help, Norbert."

He said nothing.

I waited another few seconds, then said, "What should I do?"

"Your talk to your TCQ guy, Lally. Tell me how that went."

I chose my words carefully. "He couldn't help me out with FPP. That was, and still is, my priority. He wanted to help me prevent my next FPP."

"I spoke to him. He said your conversation was brief, that you seemed reluctant to engage further but that you parted on good terms."

So Craig had kept his promise.

"When I pressed him, he said he was sure he could help you, but that you'd have to ask for help if you wanted it."

"Oh."

Norbert cleared his throat. "My advice is for you to ask for his help. Beg if you have to, but get his help."

I bit down on my lip for a moment before asking, "But why him?"

"Because frankly, I don't know anyone else who wouldn't do precisely what you've already done. I am clutching at straws here. Maybe he can see things the rest of us can't."

"But what if he can't help me?"

"Then you're no worse off." He was silent for a moment. "Maybe you should start looking for a new job, Steve. Leave under your own terms. You have a few months before things come to a head." Then he hung up.

I put the phone down and rested my head in my hands. The day had started well, but then suddenly—due to circumstances beyond my control and despite my loyalty to Wyxcomb and to my bosses—I'd become expendable.

Eventually I looked up. Five very long minutes had passed. It felt like more. I grabbed my phone, forced a smile on my face and dialed Craig Lally. It was 3:56 p.m.

CHAPTER TWENTY-THREE

Craig answered, then paused as if I'd taken him by surprise. "I didn't expect to hear from you again."

He sounded more distracted than surprised.

I apologized for how our breakfast meeting had ended, then asked him if he could please spare me thirty minutes to help me out with FPP.

"Thirty minutes? I don't have thirty minutes to spare."

"Fifteen minutes, then? It shouldn't take more than that."

"I'm afraid I am very busy just now."

I steeled my jaw. "I'm desperate. I swear I wouldn't ask otherwise."

Another pause. "Yes, okay. I'll give you ten minutes, but no more."

I thanked him. I had no intention of just sticking to my ten minutes. "We're experiencing a few little problems."

"Little problems? You said you are desperate."

"No, desperate is accurate."

I spent the first eight of my ten minutes explaining why I was so desperate, glossing over the details of the mutiny.

He summed up matter-of-factly. "So, your concern is this: Hal Gibbet, a man not known for taking prisoners, expects you to deliver FPP by December 1st, but you don't know how long it will take to build the remaining features, then test and rework them; therefore you don't know if you can keep your promise. Is that it?"

"Yes."

"The cloud we drew. Has anything changed?"

"It's the same cloud, just much worse. The date's shrunk and the only way we can possibly deliver on time—and that is very unlikely—is to cut more features and risk a shoddier, riskier product."

"That's good."

"Good? How?"

"Let's use that pressure to advantage. A noose around one's neck, they say, is very good at focusing one's thoughts." He laughed when he said it.

I didn't laugh. It was *my* neck he was talking about. At least, that's what I thought.

I told him my ten minutes was up.

"Your crisis has come at a very inconvenient time for me. But give me a few moments, okay?"

I heard his muffled voice as he carried on a conversation in the background. He was back a couple of minutes later.

"I need to make a phone call. I'll call you back."

I hung up, and three minutes later my phone rang.

"I've just spoken with Norbert. I've cleared my diary for the afternoon. I'll meet you downstairs, in the cafeteria, in twenty minutes. Bring your FPP folder with you."

CHAPTER TWENTY-FOUR

I met Craig in the cafeteria's dining area. Apart from a few folk meeting around tables the cafeteria was empty. It would be busier later when the evening shift call center workers came in early for their pre-work, subsidized dinners.

I shook Craig's hand briskly, then dropped the FPP folder on the coffee table with a *thunk* and asked him if he wanted some green tea.

"We don't have time." He gestured towards the seat across from him. "Norbert confirmed your job is at risk."

I nodded. What else could I say?

He placed his phone on the table. "He said that if you walked out on me this time, then I should ask you to call him."

"What?"

"He said he will fly here and take over your job."

I flinched. "He couldn't do my job."

Craig shrugged, then—having passed on Norbert's message—changed topic. "My son gets married this weekend. The wedding rehearsal is this evening. My family has flown in from around the world and I'm on vacation for the next three weeks. So your timing, from your point of view, sucks. From my point of view, I'm on holiday for three weeks."

I could feel the noose tighten around my neck. Out of politeness, I added, "Congratulations. We should get started then."

"Excellent!" he boomed. He stood. "Leave your folder there. Follow me."

We started walking towards the kitchen and he said, "There's just one rule I want you to follow."

"What's that?"

"Do not think about small batches. Okay?"

"Small what?"

"Batches. Don't think about them."

CHAPTER TWENTY-FIVE

Cheryl's eyes narrowed when she saw me. "You again?"

I said, "I'm sorry how our last meeting ended."

She pursed her lips and studied my face. I guess she decided that I meant what I said. "You want to hear about our French Fry Revelation?"

"I do."

"Follow me, then," she said, and led us through to her little office where the three of us sat.

"Last time, you heard how Craig forced us to eat our own dog food. That led us to test our food and fix it, at first only after it was cooked. But as we got better we learned to fix it before, during or after each stage of the cooking process. Our products' quality improved enormously. That won us loads more customers. We made loads more money. We saved our jobs. Remember?"

I nodded. She was clearly proud of the achievement.

"That was the first step," she continued. "We call the next step our *French Revelation*, which is short for French Fry Revelation. You'd be surprised how much you can learn from a few deep-fried potatoes." She chuckled at her own joke. I chuckled too, politely. A lot was hinging on this meeting.

"Our revelation helped solve two problems. First, we cooked much of our food long before we served it. So even though it tasted good fresh from the kitchen, it didn't taste so good when it hit the customer's plate." She stood up. "Come with me."

She led us out of her office and through the kitchen's swinging double doors down to the far end of the serving area. She pointed at the big shiny things where the food was stored.

"These are called bain-maries. They keep food warm after it's cooked until it is served." She pointed at a large roast of beef sitting under hot lamps. "And those lamps, they keep the roasts warm."

I nodded my understanding.

"Have you tasted two-hour-old cabbage?"

I nodded. "My Grandmother was an expert at one-hour-old cabbage."

"It's not nice, is it? Now, Steve, we used to keep our food warm using the bain-maries and heat lamps. Trouble is, if food sits too long it transforms into …"

She looked at me, eyebrows furrowing, as she waited for me to finish her sentence. I hesitated, then said, "Dog food?"

Smiling, she slapped me on the arm. "You've got a great memory, Steve."

It hurt a little, but I was still pleased with her praise.

Then she shook her head, as if disappointed. "Back then, we cooked our food in big batches. A big pot of peas. A big pot of cabbage. A big pot of carrots. They all went on at 10:30. Then, after they were cooked, we moved the food to the serving area until folks came down for their lunch. The food wasn't too bad if you ate at noon, but it was horrid at 2 p.m."

I glanced at Craig. He was listening with his head tilted to one side, as if he were hearing her story for the first time.

Cheryl said, "We used little catering tricks to prevent deterioration. Like, did you know that by adding loads more oil to a big pot of curry it will sit much longer on a low heat without burning?"

"No."

"Well, you do now. Just remember that the next time you're tempted by a cheap curry takeout."

I said I would. Then Cheryl asked me to sum up the problem she'd just described.

"Your first problem was that your food deteriorated because you cooked it too far in advance."

She nodded. "Too far advance in big …"

I looked at Craig and smiled. "In big batches. Not small batches, big batches."

"Our second problem was that on some days, especially rainy days, we didn't produce enough food and the staff complained. But other days we produced too much, and we chucked a lot of it." She turned to Craig. "Tell me again, what did you call that in industry?

Craig said, "Producing stuff that doesn't sell is called overproduction. Losing sales because you don't have what your customers want to buy is called underproduction. Overproduction wastes a lot of effort and money. Underproduction means you lose sales revenue. Both are bad, but under-producing and losing sales is usually the worst of the two."

"On some days we'd do both," Cheryl continued. "We'd cook up too much soup but not enough lasagna. We guessed at the start of each week how much to produce for the following week, and we almost always got it wrong. You can understand that, right?"

I nodded. How could you guess something like that?

"Now, Steve, do you see the obvious solutions to these problems?" Cheryl asked.

I didn't. I'd never worked in a kitchen or a restaurant. At college I tutored high school kids; the money was better than waiting tables and so were the hours, but it left fundamental gaps in my knowledge of how to reengineer a staff cafeteria.

I shook my head. "Honestly, I don't."

"That's okay. Nor did we. But thankfully, that's when we had our French Revelation." She led us back into the kitchen and over to the deep fryers.

CHAPTER TWENTY-SIX

I looked down at the deep, oil-filled fryer vats. There were three of them. We had a small domestic version at home that Mom sometimes used when cooking the kids' dinner.

"So this is where the magic happened?" I said.

"Indeed it did," said Cheryl. "Now, tell me. What would happen if we ever ran out of chips?"

"You'd all be strung up outside the castle gates."

She nodded. "Would that happen if we ran out of salad, or soup, or two-week-old cabbage?"

"Not much. Maybe people would eat chips instead."

She nodded. "Unspoken rule Number One around here is: Don't run out of chips. Rule Two is Don't serve cold chips. Understand?"

I smiled. "Some things are sacred."

"Our French Fry Revelation happened when Craig asked me why we never ran out of chips and yet, at the same time, we rarely threw out chips because of cooking too many. You know what I said to him?"

"No idea."

"It's obvious, Steve. Our serving staff keeps an eye on how many chips they've got out front, and when it gets too low, they shout out and we cook more. Craig says we *replenish on demand.* Has he asked you to not think about small batches yet?"

I looked at Craig, but he was eagerly reading a safety instruction notice stuck beside the fryers. "He has."

"He did the same to me. It was like I was an oyster and he'd planted a bit of grit inside my shell, hoping I'd turn it into a pearl. I spent a few days trying hard to not think about small batches, but of course the opposite happened. I soon figured out how to cook our vegetables in small batches. It didn't take long to sell the idea to my team, and we never looked back. It was scary at first. The first day was nuts, the second day was a little bit less nuts, and things just kept getting less nuts every day."

I said, "Is that why you have a sign out front that says that some food may contain nuts?"

She ignored me. "Nowadays, we prep most of the vegetables—clean them, peel them, wash them, slice them, dice them—before the lunch rush. We cook our first small batch just before lunch, and during the lunch service our servers keep an eye out on what's selling. They shout out to the cooks when we need to put on the next batch. With me?"

I frowned. "What happens if you're really busy? Maybe it's snowing and no one wants to leave? Don't you run the risk of the kitchen not keeping up? And all of those small batches must add overhead."

"That could happen, but it doesn't. Can you figure out why?"

I put my hand up to my chin and thought. "Do you cook in larger batches, based on demand?"

"Bingo!" she said. "Give the man a cigar!"

Strange. That was the second time someone had offered me a cigar that day.

"Our customers loved our fresher tasting vegetables—loved it!—so we figured out how to cook more food in smaller batches. You, being a computer whiz, might not realize that not all foods—soup, for instance—suffer from being cooked in big batches. Nonetheless, once we were happy with our approach to vegetables, we picked soup as the second food type to cook in smaller batches."

"I don't understand."

Cheryl smiled. She'd told her story so many times before, she'd figured out how to tell it like a mystery story. "What if you cooked up a big batch of soup at the start of the day but no one liked it?"

Oh, okay. I could see where she was going now. "People would buy it and then moan about it to their friends. You'd end up pouring the soup down the sink."

"And?"

Hmm. "And … if it happened a lot then people just wouldn't risk buying soup."

"Exactly. So we cooked a smaller batch of soup, and if it wasn't popular, we'd put on a new flavor ASAP. And if the soup was popular, then we'd cook a bigger batch of the same, pronto."

"So you must only sell soup that is quick to prepare?" I asked.

"Usually, though we do have some favorites that are safer."

I thought for a moment. "So, cooking small batches not only improved your product quality, it also solved your forecasting problem. Rather than cooking in big batches, way in advance, you cook smaller batches, which lets you adapt your menu according to what people are buying."

"Exactly!" said Cheryl. "By the end of the first month, we were serving thirty percent more customers, our revenue was up by forty percent, and since most of our costs were fixed, we were suddenly turning a healthy profit. We got to keep our jobs." She reached across to Craig and patted him on the arm affectionately. "And that not only made us happy, but proud."

I nodded. "There's one thing I don't understand. Surely switching to smaller batches meant your kitchen staff was much busier over lunchtime?"

"That's why we didn't change everything at once. And we did some clever but simple things, like changing our menu to sell food that cooked quickly and buying a few inexpensive pot dividers so we could cook one big pot of three different vegetables all at the same time. We also conducted a little clandestine commercial espionage."

Cheryl continued, smiling as she described how she and her staff took turns visiting the good High Street lunch shops and spied on them to learn how they worked. They used some of their early profits to purchase two small ovens like the ones Subway uses, and they started baking small batches of fresh lunch rolls throughout the lunch break. They replaced two bain-maries with a sandwich bar, since they no longer needed the storage space.

Her face beamed with obvious pride. "Not bad, eh?"

Craig said, "Not bad at all."

And that, it seemed, was Cheryl's story. Remove defects at the front end, build quality in, and produce small batches. All three had improved the quality of the product. Small batches also helped them cook the food customers wanted to buy rather than cooking stuff that got trashed.

It all made perfect sense.

To them.

But me? I had no idea how it applied to my situation. I didn't know what small batches meant in a software context. And I suspected neither did Craig. He may hope the principles Cheryl's team used also applied to software development, but I was certainly a guinea pig. But for the next few hours, I decided I would cross my fingers and hope he was right. I had nothing left to lose.

Craig thanked Cheryl and we made our way back to our seats out front.

We both took a minute or two to check our phones. I had a dozen low priority emails and a voice mail from Eleanor which more or less told me that she was in Malmö with Hal, that she'd spoken to Norbert, and that I was to work with Craig or pack my bags. Nice.

I powered the phone down lest she call me again, then looked up and saw Craig was waiting for me.

"There's another thing Cheryl's team did that she forgot to tell you. They thinned their menu of all but their most popular dishes. That give them wiggle room during their peak times to learn how to work their new way, and they gradually added new dishes, over time, to keep their menu interesting."

"Okay." It would be some time before I realized how important that step—thinning the menu—would be to us.

CHAPTER TWENTY-SEVEN

I took a moment or two to scan the restaurant. It was getting late in the day, and a small line of evening shift workers stood in front of the serving area. I knew they were evening shift staff because they wore comfortable, casual clothing. For some reason I'd never fathomed, formal dress was only important if you worked daylight hours. Unless, of course, you were a waitress, a bouncer or one of those old-fashioned vampires.

I stuck my hand up, like a school boy. "What next, chief?"

Craig said, "Well, we could spend a couple of hours debating whether the lessons learned in a commercial kitchen can be applied to a software environment—two very different situations, admittedly."

I nodded.

"But we don't have time. We could go through my more formal process, draw a bunch of clouds and then a few other diagrams.

I nodded again.

"But we don't have time. So, since you're desperate, we will skip the debates, skip the formal process, and instead figure out whether we can apply the lessons from Cheryl's kitchen to your type of work. Okay?"

"Okay."

"This process can take days, sometimes months. So we're going to speed things up. I warn you: This might make your ears bleed."

I sat up straight in my chair. "I'm up for it. Where should we start? With small batches?"

He frowned, then shook his head. "Before we talk about solutions we need to agree whether, conceptually and practically, you suffer the same problems."

I tilted my head forward, acknowledging his point, but thinking that there was no point talking about a solution if we'd already tried it and it didn't live up to its promise.

I said, "Before we do that, you should know that we already do an enormous amount of in-process inspection." I wasn't sure if he'd remember the details of our earlier discussion.

"You said." Then he went quiet. A minute passed, and then he smiled as if pleased with himself. "A question for you: From what Cheryl just described, did in-process inspections and testing—what we call building quality in—fully eliminate quality issues in her kitchen?"

I shook my head. "No. They improved the quality of their food further when they switched to small batches. It stopped the food deteriorating while it sat waiting to be consumed."

"Good. You were paying attention," he said, "Here's something that Cheryl didn't mention earlier. When they started cooking in smaller batches they started finding problems far sooner, when it was cheaper and easier to fix them. It's the same in factories. If there's a systemic problem in a manufacturing process that causes defects, then they'll find it far sooner if they process batches of twenty widgets, rather than two thousand. "

I said, "You keep talking about small batches, Craig."

"I know." He spoke firmly. "But don't you start thinking too much about them. Not yet."

"Is that some reverse psychology trick intended to make me think about them?"

He smiled, and I thought he looked a little embarrassed. "It is. It's a frustrating feeling, isn't it?"

"Intensely."

He pointed at the FPP folder. "Now, let's talk about forecasts."

CHAPTER TWENTY-EIGHT

"Forecasts?"

"Does your FPP project have a forecasting problem, like Cheryl's team did?"

I closed my eyes again and tried to imagine Cheryl's problem, to make it more concrete in my mind. If they forecast at the start of the week that they'd sell two hundred servings of lasagna but only sold one-fifty, then they wasted fifty servings. If they sold all two hundred, but there was demand for two-fifty, then the next fifty customers missed out, resulting in lost sales. FPP had that same problem, but on a much larger scale.

"Mark and Hal kicked off FPP based on forecasts of how well it will sell when it hits the marketplace. They did market research, surveys, studied goat entrails and tea leaves and consulted an oracle, and in the end came up with a range of sales figures. They estimated their running costs and decided FPP was a good commercial bet, and they've been crossing their fingers ever since."

Craig said, "So they still have a big Market Risk."

I nodded. "They don't know how well it will sell. And if FPP sells less than their forecasts, we're in big trouble."

"And they don't know when it will start selling either, do they?"

"No. *How well* FPP sells is not my problem, thankfully, because I can't affect that. But as you know, *when* it starts selling has become my problem."

"Tell me, do FPP's features match your future potential customers' needs?"

"I hope so, but like I said, that's beyond my control." I shrugged. "We spent a big chunk of time at the start of FPP working with Catherine's team, nailing down their requirements."

I picked up the requirements folder, turned to the last page and held it open in front of Craig so he could see my signature and Mark Richmond's signature, both of which had been captured as digital images, at the bottom of the page.

Craig nodded. "Your requirements document acts like a contract then?" He glanced at the bottom of the page. "A three hundred and twelve-page contract between you and your customers?"

I folded my arms. "Essentially."

He took the folder from me, weighed it in his hands, then flipped through the pages before handing it back to me. "Is this the original requirements document or the current requirements document?"

"The original. We descoped many of the original requirements. Our analysts use a spreadsheet now."

He pushed himself back in his chair and stretched his neck and shoulders. "These things you call *requirements*—I don't think that word means what you think it means."

I said nothing.

"If they were genuinely required"—he made little quote marks with his fingers—"then that implies they were mandatory. And if they were mandatory, then how could your customers descope them? How could they possibly be required one minute, then not required the next? They sound more like requests or guesses—as in "we think we'd like this"—rather than mandatory requirements."

Craig jabbed at the folder with his forefinger. "Here's how I see it, Steve. When your team wrote this document, it was in fact a forecast, nothing more than a prediction or an educated guess."

I shook my head. "We put a lot of effort into getting that right."

"But it wasn't right, was it?" he said. "How many times have you descoped requirements?"

"Twice."

"And the requirements that remain, do you think your customers would change them if they could?"

I nodded and thought back to the long list of change requests Gregor was working through before I told the team about Chaste's skullduggery. "Yes."

He lifted the folder and handed it to me. "Can you show me where, in this requirements document, is the requirement to ship on December 1st?"

I shook my head. "Come on, that's not fair. That's a different type of requirement."

"Fair enough." He nodded. "This document was your and your customer's forecast of what FPP could deliver, and it turned out to be incorrect. Forecasts sometimes do that."

My face felt hot—from embarrassment or anger, I wasn't sure. As much as my instincts were to fight him, he was making sense. Maybe he had a point. I exhaled, then banged my fist in the palm of my hand. "You could look at it that way ... you could say we guessed incorrectly and you'd be right ... but that's not our fault." I didn't like how awkward and defensive I sounded.

I deepened my voice. "We *had* to descope. Our customers needed us to. We couldn't deliver the product within commercially acceptable timelines otherwise. Look, you know this. I explained it to you earlier." I shook my head. "You cannot blame us for that."

His face fell away, as if I'd disappointed him. "Blame? I'm not blaming you. Things changed; you adapted. That's good. My question is, why did you build stuff that you then had to descope?"

My voice wanted to rise into a defensive whine again, but I fought it. "We had to descope because we screwed up our estimates and the project took far longer than we expected. If we had gotten the dates right, we would have cut the scope far earlier, before we'd built any of it."

"So, your end-date was a forecast too?"

"An estimate."

"Same thing."

I shook my head vigorously. "You're playing word games with me!"

"It's annoying isn't it? But the words you use are wrong, and because they're wrong they give the wrong impression and cause the wrong behaviors. Forecasts, by definition, will sometimes be right and will sometimes be wrong; otherwise we'd call them facts. Do you understand that?"

"Perhaps," I agreed reluctantly.

"Here's the lesson: You can blame yourselves when your forecasted requirements are wrong, or you can change the way you work so it matters less. I live in Scotland where it rains a lot. So, in April when the weather is particularly variable, even if the weather forecast says sunny, I still carry an umbrella."

"How do I do that? How can we build software if we can't define it clearly and unambiguously up front?"

He shook his head. "That's for you to figure out."

I slumped back in my chair, closed my eyes and thought about how Cheryl's team wasted a lot of food and disappointed a lot of customers by cooking to a forecast. They'd fixed that by making an initial short-range forecast, then cooking in small batches and changing what they cooked based on actual demand.

The French Fry Revelation.

Small batches.

I opened my eyes and looked at the requirements folder. I recalled a saying by some advertising guy who said he knew that half of his advertising budget was a waste of money, but he just didn't know *which* half. How could we possibly know, at the start of a project, which half of my requirements—or forecasts, or requests, or whatever—were less important and could be sacrificed later on, if we had to descope? Our customers only ever figured that out when things got tight and when IT resource was scarce. If only they could—and would—do that at the start.

I leaned forward in my chair. "You really aren't going to tell me the answer, are you?"

"I didn't tell Cheryl and she figured it out. And many very clever people have learned from her story since then. I'm sure you will figure it out too."

He reached across the coffee table and patted the requirements document. "This document is just over three hundred pages long, Steve. How thick would it be if your analysts rewrote it so that it matched the spreadsheet they're currently using to track your requirements?"

I shrugged, feeling momentarily defeated. "Maybe eighty pages, maybe a hundred."

His jaw dropped. "I had no idea."

"Few do."

"So you'll deliver one third of the original requirements? Wow."

"Yep," I said. Then I smiled and added. "But it is the most important third."

"Explain."

CHAPTER TWENTY-NINE

I mentally searched for an example of some of the requirements—I found it hard not to use that word—we'd cut.

"Originally we had several mechanisms for paying money to FPP's customers. The default method uses the standard inter-bank transfer mechanism. It's cheap and very easy to implement, and mandatory. Originally, Catherine's team required we be able to pay using three other methods: by check, by instant payment to their U.K. bank account, and by telegraphic transfer to an overseas account. Catherine chopped those three methods out."

He raised his eyebrows, confused. "But surely your team already built those features?"

"Built, but not yet tested. They were much harder, more time consuming, and more expensive to test than the basic option. We spent a lot of time building them, but because they're more complicated we will save a lot of time now that we don't have to test them."

"So you're throwing them away? Tossing them, just like Cheryl did with her unsold product at the end of each meal? "

I nodded. I waited for him to tell me that was called overproduction, but he didn't.

Craig frowned and rubbed his chin. "And by cutting those features, won't that make it harder to sell FPP? Won't you lose customers since the product has less features?"

"Hardly," I said, smiling at the madness of it all. "We descoped the less important features. Those features look good on a product specification sheet, but very, very few customers were ever likely to want them. Catherine said early on that we'd definitely never offer the option to pay by check.

"But why on earth would she require that feature in the first place if they're not all that valuable?"

"Scarcity."

He looked at me as if I were crazy. "Scarcity?"

"IT resource is a scarce resource. I've got a four-year-long backlog of projects waiting to be started. Whenever a new project starts, the project's customers know that they'll only ever get one shot at getting the project right, that it will be years until they get another wedge of IT resource to enhance it, so what do they do? They ask us to build every feature they can possibly think of—even if they don't think they'll ever use it."

"So the FPP developers built a check payment mechanism on the off-chance that maybe one day they needed a check payment mechanism?"

"Exactly. My eldest daughter does the same with roasted potatoes. She loves them and she worries there won't be enough; she used to pile them onto her plate, hoarding them, just in case. We stopped her doing that and asked her to just take more later, if she wants them."

Craig half-laughed, half-snorted. "Ha! She now takes them in smaller batches, based on her actual demand?"

My jaw fell open. "Oh, yes. Smaller batches."

"If it was so easy to stop your daughter's hoarding, why haven't you stopped your customers hoarding? Surely everyone knows it happens?"

"Everyone does know, and if I had my way, I'd force each of my projects' sponsors to rank each project's features and requirements, like Catherine did in our war room. Then I'd chop fifty percent of them before we even started the project. If we got lucky and finished early, then they could either go live early and we could start the next project on our big backlog, or we could use the time to layer on some of the lower value features."

"Okay, I get that. It's a bit like buying a basic model of a car, then choosing to add on extras if you had the budget," he sounded almost grumpy. "But why don't you insist that your customers prioritize at the start?"

"I've tried, but our customers insist that every single feature is top priority and therefore mandatory." I nodded towards the thick requirement folder. "And yet, in a crisis, it took less than four hours to strip those three hundred pages down to one hundred."

I paused, then added, "Hoarding is one cause of overproduction. Another is that our customers know, at the start of their project, that later on they'll be asked to chop out features, so they add stuff that they don't really want in order to protect the features they do want."

"Packing peanuts."

“Pardon?”

“They're like those foam peanuts businesses fill packages with so the goods they're shipping don't move around in transit.”

“I suppose.”

“Now, tell me, what's the equivalent of underproduction?"

It only took me a moment to figure it out. "Change requests."

"Explain."

I spoke slowly as I carefully considered my words. "Underproduction happens when we don't build something our customer wants. We don't build it, because—to use your words—we didn't forecast it at the start of the project. In my words, a requirement is wrong, so our customers ask us to change it, or a requirement is missing, so they ask us to add it."

I told him about FPP's Customer Level Income change request, the one I heard about in Gregor's management meeting just before I announced the FPP emergency. It stuck in my mind clearly. I even remembered its CR number: 191. It was a typical example.

He said, "And your customers really wanted it? They weren't just negotiating with you, playing some game?"

"Catherine said it was a real money-spinner."

"So why was it rejected?"

"Simple. Change requests take a lot of extra work, and they mostly happen near the end of the project when it's harder to change the code and we're usually already behind schedule. They chew up any contingency hidden in our plans and make us deliver late."

He said, "In the cafeteria, they lost sales and disappointed their customers when they didn't cook enough of a popular dish. In the old days, they had no ability to change their forecasted menu after 9 a.m."

I picked the requirements document up off the table and leafed through the pages. "There's some good research out there on this, Craig, and for medium to large projects, on average, we could expect a quarter to a third of the requirements in this document to be changed during the duration of the project."

"So what's that? Between seventy-five and a hundred of the original three hundred pages?"

"Uh-huh. And those are only the changes that get approved. We reject many more than that."

"And I bet your customers know that and only ask for the most important changes."

"Of course."

Craig leaned forward, then said in a soft voice. "I've got some good news and some bad news."

I leaned forward. "What's the bad news?" Though I knew what was coming.

"The bad news is that I have a wedding rehearsal to go to. I need to leave very soon or my son's wedding rehearsal will be ruined and his new mother-in-law will end up in jail for murdering me."

"And then you're not back in the office for another three weeks."

He nodded. "But I have two pieces of good news. First, I will give you some homework and then meet you here very early tomorrow morning to review it. Second, you have all the pieces of the jigsaw in your brain, and I am certain you can solve this problem."

I shook my head. "I seriously doubt that."

He ignored me and stood up. "I need to call my son, let him know I'm on my way. While I'm gone, can you draw a conflict cloud for change requests?"

"You're kidding?"

He pulled out his phone and walked away.

I sulked for a minute, feeling sorry for myself, then pulled out my pen and ripped a piece of paper from the requirements folder. Turning the page over to the blank side, I imagined the stick-man shape and drew the five boxes. I filled out the D and D' boxes easily—change vs. don't change—then I jotted down the pros and cons for each side, filled in the B and C boxes, and then the A box. It took just a few minutes.

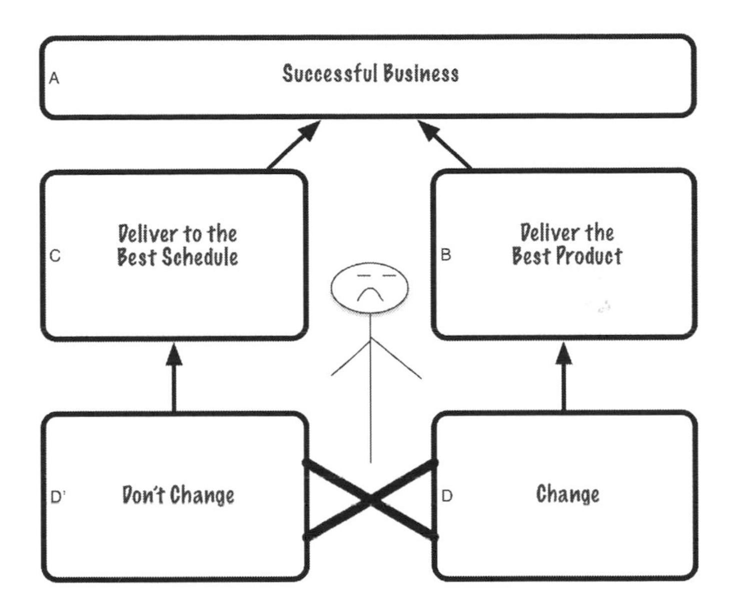

Craig soon returned, still talking on his phone, and found me winning a game of solitaire on Camilla. (Fran used to call my phone that because sometimes, she said, it was like there were three of us in our relationship.) I felt tired.

He stood in front of me, looked down, and then said to the person on the phone, "I'll ask him." He placed his hand over the microphone. "Eleanor wants to know how we're getting along. What shall I tell her?"

"Like old friends."

He repeated my words then hung up and sat down. I pushed the cloud towards him. He read it once silently, and then once more out loud.

"In order to have a commercially successful product, we must make a good product. In order to make a good product, we must approve change requests. In order to have a commercially successful product, we must deliver on time. In order to deliver on time, we must not approve change requests. Norbert said you were a quick learner."

I ignored the compliment. "How does this help me? I can't approve any change requests in FPP."

"Why not?"

I gasped. What a stupid question. "The only thing the FPP team will be doing between now and December is finding and fixing defects. We'll squeeze in as many rounds of testing as we can, but even then we will ship a shoddy product. Changes are a luxury we can't afford. We've already discussed this."

"Will you have any room to do change requests after December 1st?"

I shook my head. "Assuming we ship on time, we'll still have to spend several months fixing bugs. We won't have many customers, so while it's not ideal, it's tolerable."

"Steve, you're forgetting one thing."

"What?"

"The sad picture you've just painted is what you were going to do before we started talking. But things are different now. You have the pieces of the jigsaw puzzle in your head, and when you snap them together, you'll see a different picture."

More word games, but I played along. "What are the pieces of the puzzle?"

"You tell me."

“I don't even know what the picture on the puzzle box looks like.”

“Tell me what Cheryl did.”

So I listed off the ideas Cheryl had applied to her own problem.

I started with three ideas we were already using: testing defects out at the end (which was expensive but better than no testing) and in-process inspections and in-process testing.

Then I listed the new pieces of the jigsaw: *small batches*, *prioritizing requirements*, and finally, *building to demand*, not to forecast.

Craig said, "Now, tell me what the picture on the new jigsaw box should look like."

"I ship a good quality product on December 1st. Good quality as in low defects and our customers like it."

He said, "I know I've thrown a lot at you in the last few hours, but here's one piece of the jigsaw you might not figure out because it's counterintuitive: Sacrificing quality almost always slows things down."

I raised my eyebrows and rolled my eyes, just a little, in an easy-for-you-to-say kind of way.

He smiled. "You should look happier."

"Should I?"

"You've already identified your first two slightly smaller batches."

I studied his face, trying to tell if he was joking or not. I decided he wasn't. "I have?"

He said, "What date does your first batch end on?"

I had no idea. We'd only mentioned one date in our entire conversation, as far as I could recall and ... Oh ... my ... god.

"My first batch ends on December 1st!" —he nodded, my eyes widened—"And ... the second starts immediately afterwards!"

Snap! The construction of my jigsaw began. Was it as simple as that: thinking of a big project as a series of small projects?

He grinned. "Your homework—draw the overproduction cloud; review the cloud you drew when we first met; draw more clouds, if it helps. You'll find drawing the hands easy enough, but the shoulders will challenge you. You need them, though, so persevere, even if they make you think. Once you've done your clouds, then think about small batches."

"Okay."

"I will meet you here at 5:30 tomorrow for an impossibly early breakfast. Okay?"

I said *Okay* again, but more out of habit than anything else. My head hurt.

CHAPTER THIRTY

Years earlier, when we were newly married, Fran and I had spent many of our wintery Sunday afternoons taking long lunches with friends, visiting museums and sitting in comfy coffee shop couches reading the papers. One Sunday afternoon, the two of us visited a photography exhibition at Watt's Bridge museum. The exhibition showed a timeline of aerial photographs of Watt's Bridge. The earliest pictures were taken from biplanes, I presume, way back at the start of the 20th century; more recent pictures were taken by satellites. The exhibition had even included several photographs taken in the early stages of World War II by German flights in preparation for their planned invasion of Britain.

The dominant feature in the pictures was always the Castle. It'd been around since the 1500s, centuries before aircraft or cameras had been invented and long before Watt's Bridge was even called Watt's Bridge. The Castle walls had originally defined the city boundaries—they were built as a defensive measure. Some structures were constant throughout the pictures: the old Watt's Bridge rail bridge, the upper- and middle-class Victorian housing.

But other features, like the new Watt's Road Bridge, acres and acres of residential builds, schools, motorways and two new hospitals, had popped up in the pictures bit by bit during the decades. Our local Tesco supermarket sat in the exact same spot as a World War II ammunition factory once had. Many of the poorer Victorian tenements were bulldozed during the 1960s and 1970s, their residents unceremoniously moved to the ghastly, modern high-risers, many of which have since been dynamited.

Things change.

That, I guess, is the nature of life.

If you looked carefully, you could clearly identify my house in many of the photographs. Once upon a time it was the gatehouse of a great estate, owned by Fran's ancestors. Their financial fortunes faded after World War II, and although Fran's family technically still owns the mansion and grounds, they are now a tourist attraction which all Watt's Bridge could enjoy Tuesdays through Sundays and bank holiday Mondays.

To find our home, all you had to do was look for a big green patch in the northwest corner of Watt's Bridge, identify the mansion house in the middle of that, and then follow the tree-lined lane out past the cemetery to the old coast road. And that's where we lived, in our old stone house almost hidden among the ancient trees that bordered the estate, just a few hundred yards from the sea and Fran's grave. If they ever re-run that exhibition, you'd see a trampoline and swing set in our back yard, where my kids and their friends played whenever they could, and Mom's granny flat (though we weren't ever allowed to call it that).

Things change.

That is the nature of life.

These were the things I thought about while I drove home following my conversation with Craig. I'd tried snapping more pieces of the jigsaw puzzle together, but I was too tired. And sometimes it was just nice to think of Fran and the life we had back then, the life we planned.

I parked my car and climbed out, then paused to admire the Mansion building in the distance—a habit I had developed over the years. The building was normally closed at that time of day, but there was a lot of activity on its costal side, where I saw a group of people assembling marquees. I also spotted, through the trees bordering our property, a dozen or so Scouts marching across the estate grounds. I slammed the car door shut and went inside, hungry, tired, and bewildered—but surprisingly enthusiastic about life. What a day I'd had.

I found Mom in the kitchen tossing a salad for our dinner. She'd already put the kids to bed but said Ashley, my seven-year-old sweetheart, was likely to still be reading if I wanted to kiss her good night. I went upstairs to do just that, and before I knew it the kiss had been negotiated into a kiss, a cuddle, and a chapter from one of her sickly pink fairy books. I gave her a final kiss, tucked her in, turned her lights out and closed the door. Then I popped into my bedroom where I changed into something more comfortable. As I walked out onto the landing, Alison, three years younger than Ashley but still awake, shouted out, "Night-night, Daddy."

I went in to say *night-night* and give her a cuddle. She told me a joke: *Where does chocolate mousse come from?* (She pronounced it moooooos). I gave up. *Chocolate Cows!*

I laughed disproportionally, said *night-night* again, then headed down to the kitchen where Mom was grating Parmesan cheese.

I had thought we were having Parmesan chicken, but it turned out that Mom had changed her mind and instead decided to cook one of my other favorites, mushroom risotto. Such is the nature of evening meals. Mom cooked the risotto the non-traditional, no-fuss way: in a non-stick wok, which took a whole lot less stirring, and as far as I could tell, tasted just as good. I poured us each a glass of New Zealand Pinot Gris while Mom served up the food. As we ate I told her about my day. She sat patiently listening to me, nodding appropriately and asking the right questions in the right places.

Once I'd finished, she asked me, "How much faith do you have in this Craig fellow?"

"Ummmm ... he comes highly recommended by Norbert."

"I don't want you getting your hopes up."

"Yeah, I know."

"You know, Steven," she said, reaching across and resting her hand on mine, "things might not work out. You don't need the money, but you do need to work. You've always needed to work. It's who you are. I want you to follow Norbert's direction and consider your other options, while the timing is right. If you need to commute to Edinburgh or Glasgow, then, well, we'll make that work somehow."

I snorted and waved the problem away with my hand. I wasn't ready to give up on FPP yet.

"I'll be okay."

Mom shook her head and made her serious face. "You need to protect yourself and your family. You need to start looking at other options."

I laughed, trying to hide my discomfort with this turn in conversation. "I could stay at home and look after Alison until she goes to school next year." I looked at her to see her reaction. "That would free up your time a bit, too."

Her face hardened. "Would you really do that? Really? I know you love your kids enormously, but is that really something you want to do?"

I looked down at the table and shook my head, chastened. We both knew that would never work. I'd go stir-crazy with no work to keep me busy.

"In that case," she continued, "you better do your best to make your FPP project succeed. And, tomorrow, no matter what, you call your friend Graeme." I made a face. Graeme worked for a high-end recruitment company in Glasgow. We went to university together. "Call him tomorrow. Wyxcomb will never be as loyal to you as you are to it."

"I, my ..." I stammered. "My loyalty isn't just to Wyxcomb. It's to the people I work with, my entire team. If FPP fails then Wyx-Fin won't be a happy place.

"Oh, my poor darling." She shook her head with that disappointed look only a mom can do, then spoke to me harshly. "It's Miss World's and Superman's jobs to save the world, not yours. I had hoped you'd grown out of that by now. You need to look out for yourself, and your family."

With that she got up from the table and went to her apartment—her granny flat— at the back of the house. I started the cleanup.

CHAPTER THIRTY-ONE

Mom and I had a deal: She cooked, I cleaned. She was good at cooking and I was not; she didn't like cleaning up and I enjoyed it. And our home, while big enough for us, was old. Some parts of it—like the kitchen—were tiny, and there was only room to fit one person at a time comfortably.

I cleared the table then flipped through the radio until it played a song I recognized.

I went back to the sink and started scrubbing away on the evening's dishes. Within moments I'd switched into autopilot, freeing my mind to play back my very busy day. The day had started well, then deteriorated into a mutiny and ended up with a most unusual tour of the staff cafeteria.

And, unless I pulled off a miracle, I wouldn't have a job in a few months.

Not your typical day at the office.

I'd also been assigned homework—something that hadn't happened in nearly twenty years. Best get on with that ...

The hands were simple: On the one hand, we should build as many features as possible from the requirements document, even though many were of disputable value; on the other hand, we should only build the highest value features—those that were indisputably required. I figured out the shoulders easily enough, without needing to list pros and cons: Build the best product and deliver to the best schedule. I decided the head of the cloud should be *A Successful Business.*

I stopped washing for a moment and spoke the conflict out loud.

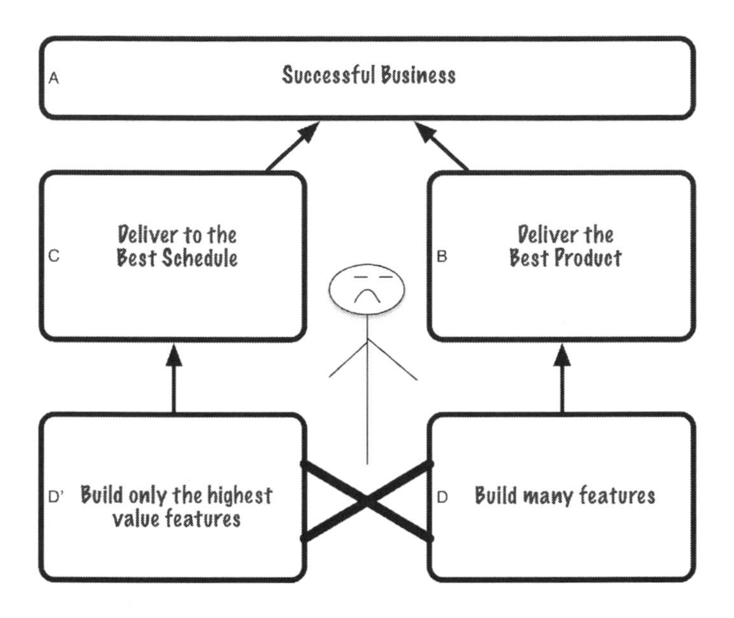

"In order to have a successful business, we must build the best product. In order to build the best product, we must build many features."

"In order to have a successful business, we must deliver to the best schedule. In order to deliver on the best schedule we must build only the highest value features."

It felt like it hung together, and I noticed how closely this conflict resembled those on the change request cloud—the head and shoulders were the same, but the hands differed. In both cases we wanted the best product and the best schedule. But because we had set out to build a big product with no real idea of how long it would take, we had achieved neither.

Like most things in the kitchen, the dish rack was small, and so it was soon full. I grabbed a fresh dish towel and quickly did the drying, then started washing again.

I considered where to go next with the cloud diagram, and I

remembered that Wyx-Health had tackled their outsourcing cloud by listing the pros and cons and then challenging them, either by showing that they were invalid, or by changing things so they were invalid. I'd skipped listing the pros and cons and jumped straight to the conflict's shoulders, so I decided to go back and do them, starting with the small product/short schedule side of the cloud.

I considered the statement: In order to deliver to the best schedule we must build only the highest value features

What were the pros of delivering a small product? It was easier to build, easier to test, and simpler to use. You got to market faster and pulled revenue in sooner. And I often preferred buying simpler products because they were easier to understand. In business terms, that must mean they were occasionally easier to sell (yet another pro), though not always. That wasn't the Wyx-Fin way, but wasn't Chaste's approach based around that idea?

I thought it interesting that some of the pros weren't just about the schedule. They also concerned the product and the flow of benefits. So the full benefit would be the ability to deliver a better product, sooner.

Sticking with the same side of the cloud, I considered the cons of the opposite hand: including many features in the product

There were many. We would build big, bloated products, full of features no one wanted. Those products would be hard to support, and while our projects lasted months and years, our products lasted decades, so big products were expensive to own.

Then I ran back over the list I had just made. Were there any invalid pros or cons, or any that I could somehow make invalid?

I couldn't find anything. There were a lot of benefits of building smaller products, those with only the highest value features and that would get to market sooner. That fit with my intuition that I'd get more leverage blitzing the other arm—the one that included all the requirements. But then again, the Wyx-Health solution had been contrary to my intuition. And how on earth did we figure out exactly what those highest value features were? Time to look at the cloud's other arm.

In order to build the best product, we must include as many features as possible, even if some were of disputable value.

What were the pros?

This was harder for me to figure out. I tried putting myself in Catherine's shoes. Why would she say something was required when it wasn't? Simple answer: because it might be, but she didn't know yet. If she didn't include it, but realized later she needed it, the only way she had to get it was to submit a change request and then do a lot of formalized begging. Odds of getting the change request approved? Lowish. It was easier for her to chuck everything in she could think of and claim they were all of high value, because she didn't know which features actually were.

So pro number one was: Features of uncertain value are more likely to be built. (But so are features of low-value).

Often, some lesser value requirements are left out in the first phase with the assurances to the customer that they will be added in during phase two, when we know more. That was a gap-filling approach: Build something, ship it, figure out what the important gaps were, then fill them in phase two.

But the odds of actually getting a phase two? Very low. Phase two was normally used to fix bugs which either weren't found or weren't fixed during the testing phase.

Catherine knew how the industry worked. She knew that FPP would never have a genuine phase two—one that was used to enhance, rather than fix, a product. And why was there no phase two? Because IT resource was too scarce. There was a more complicated answer too: It was scarce because we spent too much time building low value features. And why were those low value features being built? Because the projects didn't have a true, product-enhancing phase two, which made it safer for our customers to limit the scope of what went into phase one. I believe that is what they call a vicious circle.

Two more pros came to mind, neither of them needing much consideration: Including extra features resulted in a bigger budget and a bigger piece of the scarce IT pie, and low value features could be descoped, without losing much, when the need arose. Add those two together and you build a project with contingency—wiggle room—to absorb some overruns and some change requests.

I spoke aloud to the dishes again, trying to organize my thoughts. "There is a natural priority within our customers' requirements. They only say everything is top priority because they feel compelled to hoard." I nodded, liking what I heard.

"There must be a way to get our customers to prioritize. If I can do that, then I can break the vicious circle and break this conflict."

I nodded again. I liked where this was heading. But first, to be complete, I needed to look for the cons of the conflict's other hand: including only the highest value features—those that were indisputably required.

That was easy. We sold our products based on the features in them. If we only included the must-have features, we might find it hard to sell. That would be bad. If our competitors' products had more features, the reasoning went, then their product was clearly better and people would buy it rather than ours.

So, since we sell features and our customers buy features, the first con of reducing features was that our products would be harder to sell.

I looked around the kitchen and decided that the con must be possible to invalidate. The scrubbing brush I held in my hand did one thing and it did it well. My refrigerator kept stuff cold, and I didn't want much more from it than that (other than perhaps making a Star Trek *whisssshhh* sound when the doors opened). Other things in the house had plenty of extra features I never used. My microwave was a tiny little thing we used to defrost and reheat, though when they first came out they were sold as super-dooper oven replacements, with all sorts of whiz-bang features. The remote control with its many unused buttons. Same with the TV—I couldn't tell you what it said on the spec sheet when I bought it, but I could tell you that we could watch TV shows on it and that the mute button was worn out.

Why did we buy things based on the number of features, even if we rarely use them? Was it because that's how businesses sold things? Was that the only way?

I thought of Chaste again: They didn't sell feature-loaded products; they sold simple products with just enough features that were easy to understand and easy to use and easy to buy. Their products sold to eighty percent of customers, even though they only had twenty percent of the features.

And then that question again: How did we figure out exactly what the highest value features were?

CHAPTER THIRTY-TWO

I went to the lounge looking for any nomad dishes in need of a good cleaning and found two bowls the kids had left there after their supper. One was empty, the other half-full of soggy cornflakes. That would be my little Ashley—she always took more cereal than she needed, then we ended up wasting it. I'd asked her, many times, to just take a small bowl's worth of cereal then get more if she was still hungry, but she was still young.

I took them and an apple core I found on a side table back through to the kitchen.

I threw the apple core in our small compost bin, then washed the bowls and started on my next batch of washing. As I started scrubbing the frying pan, my mind soon turned to requirements, or *forecasts*, as Craig called them.

I'd had a few hours to cogitate on that thought, and finally I felt primed and ready to tackle the topic consciously. I decided he was rightish: Some requirements were required, but some were optional and some were guesses.

In our War Room, Catherine had already pared FPP back to the bare bones requirements. She said we couldn't go live without them, and I believed her. The default payment method I'd told Craig about, which used the United Kingdom's standard inter-bank transfer mechanism, was a good example. It was indisputably required because no one would buy the product if we didn't offer it. They were like French fries in the cafeteria.

But what about the other three payment methods she had descoped as well? They were optional, and when push came to shove, Catherine had pushed and shoved them aside. But it didn't make sense to call them *optional requirements*. That was an oxymoron, wasn't it? I needed a better word than requirements, but there were too many to choose from: solutions, designs, features, behaviors, functions, use cases ...

I flipped a coin in my head, and before it landed I'd decided to call them features. I imagined a conversation with a customer:

Me: We've built these features already.

Customer: Good. What about those other features?

Me: We haven't built them yet.

The word seemed to fit.

I paused for a moment and realized that I'd been so caught up in thinking that I'd stopped cleaning up. I poured some more hot water into the sink and started again.

So, there were four payment method features, one of them required, three optional. But here's where things got interesting: They weren't equally optional.

Of those three optional payment methods—check, instant payment to a U.K. bank account, and telegraphic transfer to an overseas account—the first, paying by check was optional and very low priority. Wyx-Fin stopped sending check payments out years earlier. It was probably included at the start of the project so that customers wise to the way of projects could look suitably pained when they agreed they could live without it during some descoping exercise. It was filler, like a bodyguard, willing to throw itself in front of a bullet to save the rich guy.

The instant payment feature was optional, but it wasn't just filler. Wealthier customers, the ones we wanted to attract, would prefer to use it for unusually large and urgent, one-off payments. It wasn't required, but I imagine Catherine would have kept it in if she possibly could have. So, it was optional and either high or medium priority.

The telegraphic transfer was the most interesting of the three. It would appeal to potential customers who would retire to Spain, say, to avoid rickets and scurvy in their later years. They would be a small subset of our wealthier and most profitable customers, and it might help our overall sales. Or it might not. We wouldn't know until we tried to sell it. Of the four options, it most resembled a forecast. Its value was uncertain. If there were a phase two and we discovered demand for it, then we would build it to fill that gap.

I stopped and smiled to myself. I felt like I'd just realized what I'd subconsciously known all along.

I gave the pan an angry scrub. It annoyed me that my customers always claimed that every feature was required, when logic said they were not.

I stopped cleaning for a moment as the obvious occurred to me. If we could get our customers to prioritize honestly, then we could reduce hoarding significantly and free up scarce IT capacity. If we created more IT capacity, we'd be able to create space that would reduce the need to hoard. I guess we'd call that a *virtuous* circle.

In fact, if we could just guarantee that each project had a phase two, then we'd be halfway there. But, of course, what customer in their right mind would believe that guarantee?

I grabbed another pot from the stove, dunked it in the hot soapy water and started scrubbing. Mom had used this pot to make tomorrow morning's porridge, and even though she'd soaked it, the inside base was thick with stuck-on porridge. Ick.

As I scrubbed the pot, I realized that the word *features* didn't quite cut it. We also had some non-functional requirements—that is, requirements that were not features. They were things like security and performance and scalability—the kinds of things you measured on a scale and could have more or less of. You could have faster performance—at a price—and you could have high levels of security—also at a pricc. And you could build a system so it was easier, or harder, to scale. So the equivalent of saying that features were required or optional, when dealing with non-functionals, was the flexibility of paying for different performance level. It was like having the option of paying for a three-star hotel or a five-star hotel. They both provided the same functionality, but you paid more or less for different levels of quality.

I moved to the non-stick wok and gave it a quick brush and dry. Another word for non-functional requirements was *qualities*, which was short for qualities of service. I decided to use that word going forward, along with features, and forgo the word *requirements* for good.

Was there another way to get our customers to prioritize? It seemed to be the key.

In the cafeteria's kitchen they prioritized by cooking more of what their customers were buying. I couldn't just cook up a batch of features cheaply and make more if they sold well. That was one way our two domains were very different.

I'd told Craig how, if only our customers prioritized their features at the start of each project, we could build a smallish version of the solution, just big enough that we could comfortably deliver it before the delivery date and within budget. Then, if we had time and budget left over, we could add on their next highest features.

That sounded a lot like cooking up a medium sized batch followed by a few smaller sized batches. Craig had refused to tell me what small batches looked like in my environment. He said I'd figure it out. And, I thought I just had.

Could working in small batches be something as simple as breaking that medium sized project down into a bunch of smaller projects? Craig had grinned when I asked him that question, but not answered.

I thought it could.

Was that all there was to it?

I thought a moment, and decided it was. A small batch was a small project in which we delivered a small selection of features; not just a small selection, but a small selection of the most important features.

How disappointingly dull. I'd expected thunderclaps and awe, or maybe a Eureka Moment where I jumped out of my office and ran naked down the street. But there was none of that. Did Cheryl have similar thoughts of underwhelmed-ness when she figured out she shouldn't cook a huge pot of cabbage, but a few smaller pots? Probably.

Still, it felt right and it felt good. I smiled and told myself out loud, "Nice."

So, small batches were small projects. But that still didn't help me with the prioritization problem.

Or did it? We couldn't get our customers to prioritize adequately when we did big projects. Would they behave differently if, instead of asking them to set in stone twelve months of work, we asked them to tell us what features they needed in the first month? What if we added that our analysts, designers, developers and testers were ready to start work, and if they didn't tell us what to work on, we'd choose on their behalf and start spending their budget?

What if we added that we were most likely to pick the features that were the most technically interesting, unless they told us otherwise?

Yes. Small batches would force our customers to prioritize.

I let that thought linger …

I wiped around the benches and the kitchen table and went into the utility room to grab our broom. I gave the kitchen floor a quick sweep then emptied the rubbish bin.

Craig was right; small batches were key. But a key is useless without someone to put it in the lock, turn it, and then yank the door open.

I rushed through to the hallway and grabbed Camilla from my jacket.

CHAPTER THIRTY-THREE

Do you know any ex-smokers who only found the impetus to give up smoking after surviving their first heart attack?

I know two.

FPP was in a state of emergency—my equivalent of a heart attack survivor—and I had to make the most of that.

I dialed Catherine's number, but it went to voice mail after the tenth ring. I had just turned to walk back towards the kitchen when my own phone rang.

Without looking at the screen to see who was calling, I pushed the green button and put the phone to my ear. "Catherine. Could you have told us what FPP's minimum viable solution was—the bare bones solution from the War Room—way back at the start of the project?

She didn't even pause for breath or tell me off for calling her after hours. "Of course."

"Can you roll forward to December, after FPP is live? Can you tell me what we should be working on next?"

"Sure, my team has put together a spreadsheet of all our potential post-implementation work." She quickly rattled off the top half dozen features that came to mind. "I've a copy of the spreadsheet on my laptop. If you give me a minute I can tell you exactly what they are."

"Sure."

"But first, is FPP doomed? Vrinda said you're working on a

plan, but she didn't sound confident."

"I am working on a plan." When I heard my own voice I was surprised at just how confident I sounded. "Now, can you get me that list of features?"

While I waited, I walked across to my office at the other side of the house. I fired up my laptop, connected to the Wyx services and opened up the same spreadsheet. My laptop got there about twenty seconds sooner than Catherine's. I used the time to scan through the list of features. I wasn't really interested in what they were, but I needed to hear why Catherine had chosen those features and why she ordered them as she did.

A few moments later she started talking through the features, starting with those we hoped to tackle in December.

When she'd finished, I said "Could you have given me that list back when FPP was first kicked off?"

She took a moment. "Maybe. The essence of the list would have been similar, but the details would have been fuzzier because we hadn't worked them out yet."

"You've learned a lot about the product since we started, then?"

"Of course."

I thanked her again, then asked if she could spare me a few more minutes.

"What else would I, a good-looking single woman in the prime of my life, be doing in the evening? Having a social life?"

I ignored her sarcastic comment, and instead asked her to describe her rationale when ranking FPP's features in the War Room.

I scrolled to the top of the spreadsheet and listened as she worked her way from the top-most feature down, explaining as she went why each feature was more important than the one below it.

As Catherine talked, I recalled how I explained complicated slideshows by revealing concepts bit by bit, building the idea up over time and taking care not to overwhelm my audience with too much info. Then I thought of how Ron's support and maintenance team built up our product in the same way: They started with an existing system and then added to it bit by bit, one change request at a time.

And then another piece of my puzzle revealed itself. How was Ron McKnight able to reschedule his CORETRAN work to suit FPP's new release date so easily?

That was easy: Ron was flexible because he kept his list #2—

the requests currently being worked on—nice and short and he never made commitments about the work on his list #1—the work not yet started—until he could reasonably do so. His customers knew that, and given the scarcity of CORETRAN resources, accepted it. Limiting the number of requests on list #2 limited his work in process, which was very much like working in small batches.

I listened as Catherine continued talking, describing how the system would grow feature upon feature upon feature.

And then the most important piece of the jigsaw revealed itself from across the room; the piece that helped me see the whole picture. A newspaper, neatly folded and sitting on the edge of a couch, with the front page headline clearly above the fold. "More Factories Close: Can Jobs Blow be Reversed?" I didn't need to read the rest of the article to know what it was about. That was the clever way reporters wrote articles. They put the most important stuff at the top, and then the next most important and then the next. It gave them and their editors huge flexibility.

I thanked Catherine for her time. She asked me why I was suddenly asking all these questions. Had I known Hal was going to pull the rug out on us like that? Was there a problem she should know about? How many days had I been working on the new plan?

I told her I would explain everything the following day. Or maybe the day after that. I hung up and went into the lounge and stood beside my bookcase. I needed to find a book.

Moments later, Mom arrived carrying a small plate of cheese and nuts, in case I was still hungry. She stood behind me. "What are you looking for?"

"A book."

"What book?"

"A book about marketing and communications. It's important."

I ran my hand along the books on the first shelf of the bookcase. It wasn't there.

Mom asked me if I'd like some cheese. I said that I would, maybe, in a few minutes.

I checked the second shelf.

"Some nuts, then?"

"Maybe later." I scanned the third shelf. Plenty of books, but not the one I wanted.

"I may take a lover. Perhaps two," Mom said.

"Uh-hum," I said. How could it not be here? I checked the next two shelves, touching each book.

"Younger men, with stamina."

Okay, I heard that all right. I stopped thinking and gave her my full attention.

"What?"

"What's the book called?" she smiled. She knew she had me.

"It's called *Made to Stick*. It's got a story in it about the telegraph system."

"Is it in the attic?"

I paused, then dashed up the stairs to the landing.

I heard Mom follow me up the stairs. I reached up and turned the attic trapdoor latch open with my fingertips, then carefully let the door drop open.

"Is something wrong?"

"Nothing's wrong. Trust me. Everything is about to fall into place."

She frowned, not understanding.

I spoke with hands emphasizing the important bits. "Look, Ron's team works on lots of little projects. He ships new software several times each month. He's got three lists, each made up of different requests—bug fixes, small and medium sized enhancements—and they deliver a constant stream of filled requests. Every few days, *bam!* Another request shipped. Start the next one. Then a few days later—*bam!*—another one."

She clearly wasn't keeping up with my explanation, but I kept going anyway. I needed to hear the words spoken out loud to sanity-check them. "And then, when the FPP thing happened, Ron said he could change his release dates just like that, without any hassle. His team is so much more nimble, more responsive than all my other project teams.

"And how come he can work that way and we can't? Because his workload is made up of loads of small requests. His team completes each request, tests the arse off it, makes sure they haven't broken anything and then release it. Sometimes they release just one request at a time, sometimes they batch up several requests—it all depends on what makes sense. But they never do big batches, never." My hands were flying all over the place.

I stopped. "You see?"

She said, "I don't like it when you say the word arse, Steven."

Well, at least she was listening. I apologized, then stood on my tiptoes and reached for the attic ladder.

Mom asked me to be careful, otherwise I'd wake the kids.

I nodded and carefully pulled the ladder down to its full height. It clicked into place.

"But with FPP, it's a big project right? It's not made up of loads of little requests, right? Or, at least, that's what we thought. We thought we couldn't do what Ron does. That's what we thought. But we can. At least I think we can. Do you see?"

"I haven't got a clue what you are talking about. Just don't wake the kids. They'll be grumpy in the morning, otherwise."

"Okay. Look, there's a book in the attic. It's about marketing and it has a bit in it about journalism. It'll make things clearer."

"Journalism?"

Sometimes I worried that my mother didn't understand me. Perhaps it was a generational thing. Perhaps it was because I was speaking gibberish.

I climbed up into the attic and turned on the light. In the far corner I saw a pile of cardboard boxes full of old books. I carefully made my way across the attic, dodging two old PCs, an ancient VCR, a broken-down printer and several vacuum-packed plastic bags full of old baby clothes, until I reached the boxes. I rooted around in them until I found the book I was looking for.

When I picked my way back through the junk and back down the ladder, Mom was still there, watching me. Perhaps to make sure I didn't start reading too loudly and wake the kids. I flipped through the pages and almost immediately found what I wanted.

That was when I had what I would later realize was my own French Fry Revelation.

Except it was probably more geographically accurate to call it my Egyptian Revelation.

I knew I would need Craig's help to round out the details of my solution. I'd need Phil's help, and Ron's too, to fine-tune it.

I turned the page towards Mom and smiled at her. "There it is: the inverted pyramid."

THREE WEEKS LATER
Wednesday, September 6th
FPP launch date - December 1st, this year

CHAPTER THIRTY-FOUR

Catherine clicked the Finish button and the cursor turned into an hourglass.

Her PC desktop projected on the conference room wall.

We watched and we waited.

Ten of us sat squished around the conference table; another dozen stood against the walls. The room looked busier, more lived in, than it had three weeks earlier. The walls were covered in printouts, sticky notes and drawings. More a working room now than a War Room or a meeting room. A large fluorescent pink, green and white striped toy snake, which Vrinda had named Fippy the Snake, had mysteriously threaded his way across the top of the projection screen frame. His tongue cast a silhouette on the screen.

Catherine wore a paper hat with CSR written on it in thick black pen. CSR stood for Customer Service Representative. She would soon recruit dozens of CSRs to work in FPP's call center, but that day she was pretending to be one. She had just keyed her first customer application form into the software, and we watched and waited for the dialog box confirming that the transaction had completed successfully. I'd seen it work twice the day before, but I was still nervous. Our team's confidence, my credibility, our collective future … a lot was riding on this thin slice of FPP software working properly.

***

Three weeks earlier, I'd met Craig for a very early breakfast and explained my Egyptian Revelation—the inverted pyramid—to him in detail. When I asked if that was what he'd expected, he'd shrugged and said he knew I'd come up with something, as long as I was desperate and tried hard to not think about small batches. He told me to keep him in the loop and to ask for help whenever I needed it, except for the next three weeks while he was "off the grid." I said I would, but he looked skeptical. Which was understandable, considering how I'd avoided his help earlier, before I was desperate.

Later that morning, I'd assembled Catherine and the rest of FPP's leadership team in the conference room. It was my job to cause everyone in the room (but mostly Catherine) to feel as desperate as I had. I needed Catherine to realize that the only way she could get what she wanted was to radically slice and dice FPP's features even further than she already had.

As everyone sat, Phil smiled and leaned in close to me so no one else could hear. "There's a rumor going around that Hal had you fired."

I shook my head. "Not yet." Then I turned to face everyone. "We cannot deliver FPP on December 1st."

Silence. I made eye contact with everyone sitting around the table, but I couldn't tell if they were sad or angry or … relieved?

Tim finally answered. "February was a stretch. December is impossible."

Vrinda said, "We are on a Death March."

I nodded.

Catherine looked at me, eyebrows raised expectantly. "But you're working on a plan, right? That's what your phone call was about, right?"

"I've been working with Craig Lally, a senior TCQ consultant, over the last few weeks"—which was, technically true—"and we identified a tweak to our existing test processes that will increase our odds of succeeding."

Catherine frowned. "Increase our odds?"

"Honestly, I know this will make things better, but I do not know if we will make this new date."

I stood and walked to the back of the room. I picked six sticky notes, representing Catherine's highest priority features, from the wall. I took the notes to Catherine and asked her to read them out loud.

When she had read them aloud for everyone, I turned to Gregor. "Hypothetically, how long would it take to deliver a product containing only those six features?

Gregor reached across and took the sticky notes. He screwed up his face, studied them, then shook his head. "I don't really know." He gestured around the table. "We'd need to plan in more detail, but it would certainly take more than two weeks, if we got lucky. And maybe six or seven weeks if we don't."

Catherine's face dropped. She started to say something, which if I'd been her would have been *Why then, did you say you could deliver the entire project on February 1st when you can't even predict how long it will take to deliver these six features?* But I held my hand up and asked her to hold her fire.

I went to Gregor and took all but one of the sticky notes from him. "How long would it take to deliver just that one?"

He looked miserable. "Look, Steve, this is unfair. There's too much uncertainty. Too many things we can't know until we try."

Catherine turned to Gregor, eyes glaring. Once again, I asked her to wait just one more moment. Please.

I turned back to Gregor. "I know that's unfair of me, Gregor. Tell me though, you'd be able to deliver it by the 1st of December?"

"Almost certainly."

I feigned surprise. "You mean definitely, don't you?"

He said, "Well, almost definitely then."

This time I didn't hold Catherine back.

"Why the hell, then, did you commit to us to deliver the entire project on February 1st if you can't even tell me how long it will take you to deliver that one little feature?" She spun and looked directly at me. "I thought you guys were supposed to be professionals."

"Professionals!" blurted Gregor. "You guys upstairs wouldn't even know about Chaste's ambush if it weren't for Phil. How much money did Mark promise the Future Perfect product would deliver into Hal's coffers, based on being first to market? How do *you* have the nerve to call *yourselves* professionals?"

"Oh right, blame us for this mess," spat Catherine. "What this boils down to is that you, Gregor, made a promise to us which we took in good faith, and used in our forecasts. You know the difference between my promise and your promise? My promise was to

Mark Richmond and Hal Gibbet. You're screwing around with my career here,"—she took a deep breath—"not to mention Wyx-Fin's reputation and profitability."

It seemed like a good time to intervene. "I made that promise, Catherine, not Gregor. And I admit I've had my fingers crossed since, hoping I'd make good on it. We haven't. I'm sorry."

"Well, I'm sorry, too, Steven," said Catherine, her eyes narrowed, "But if you, or Gregor, or whoever is running this joint can't even commit to delivering that one feature, then I've got to go back to Mark and advise to scrap the entire frigging project." She sat right back in her chair, folded her arms and muttered something my mom wouldn't have approved of.

To my surprise, Vrinda jumped to Gregor's defense. "Gregor did not say he couldn't deliver that one feature by December 1st. He said he couldn't promise to with certainty. There are a few things that could go wrong—earthquakes, fires, floods, all jump to mind—but they're very unlikely to happen."

Phil stuck his hand up as if asking permission to speak. Really, though, he was my plant and he was asking if it was a good time to throw in a comment he and I had discussed before the meeting. I nodded.

"Realistically, it is more likely that the messaging technology will blow up in our face," Phil said.

The whole room turned to look at him. The word *aghast* springs to mind. I could tell everyone was wondering why he hadn't ever mentioned this before.

"Hey, it's in your risk register," he said, seemingly surprised at our reactions. "It looked okay during proof-of-concept, way back when, but it's never been tested. We're guinea pigs. We all knew that."

Catherine folded her arms tightly. "So, what you're saying is, we won't know if it's an issue or not until we start testing?"

At the word *testing*, Tim stepped in. "The project is loaded with question marks, things we can't know until we test. The messaging system is top of our list."

Catherine unfolded her arms. "That's why we test, right?"

"Of course."

Catherine let out a deep breath. "Here's my problem: I have to know if this project has legs or not. The messaging system could kill us, and we need empirical evidence one way or the other. So you need to start testing it today."

"You're right," I said. "We must start testing as soon as possible. But we need to start testing more than just the messaging system. And we can't wait until the testing phase starts."

"What do you mean?"

I nodded at Phil.

He stood up, collected the six sticky notes from the table in front of him, and then stuck them back on the wall. We all watched as he stood and stared at the wall. After a minute or so, he picked up one of the sticky notes.

He spoke directly to Catherine. "We have to test this feature eventually, and let's be honest, rework it. There's no way it's going to work right the first time. Problem is, the testing phase doesn't start for another few weeks." He took a deep breath and exhaled it slowly. "The good news, Catherine, is we *can* pull some specific bits of testing forward, and start testing them now."

He nodded slowly to himself. "We could start doing that tomorrow, maybe even later today. If the testing uncovers bad news, then good! We've found it early, when there is more time to fix it. If it doesn't, then even better. We go back to business as usual."

Gregor stood and joined Phil at the wall, which pleased me. Phil was my accomplice, but Gregor was following his intuition. He peeled off another sticky and said we should do the same with the feature it represented. He said it contained nasty CORETRAN changes which weren't tested yet.

Soon, everyone but me was standing at the wall. I sat back and watched them chat for another fifteen minutes before they finally agreed to spend the next week or so testing and reworking three of the riskier high-value features.

The team rejoined at the table, and I asked if everyone felt better about the project now. They looked at each other and nodded.

"We will learn a lot about the quality of our earlier work," Catherine said.

Gregor added, "And in a week or so, we will have a far better idea of whether we can hit December 1st or not."

I nodded in what I hoped was a thoughtful manner. "Agreed. We start the testing phase today, with those features as our first small batch. But there's more to it than that. I need to tell you about the outcome of my discussions with Craig Lally, from the TCS group.

"My light bulb moment hit me last night as I was talking with Catherine." I looked at Catherine, and she smiled. "It wasn't a classic light bulb moment like you read about other geniuses having." (Perhaps implying I was a genius was a little over the top, but I felt rather pleased with myself.) "No apple fell on my head, no water spilt in my bath. It was more like when you're catching a 6 a.m. flight and you switch your bedroom light on to stop yourself from going back to sleep after your alarm goes off."

I chuckled, genius-like.

No one laughed back.

"So," I continued, "way back in the nineteenth century, journalists invented a new way of writing newspaper articles. It's called the inverted pyramid. It allowed reporters to keep their commitments under conditions of high uncertainty. Let me tell you their story."

I asked them to imagine that they were a reporter out in the Wild West somewhere, and they'd just gotten a hot news story that they needed to send to their editor in New York. Before the telegraph came along, they'd have written their story then sent it off to the editor—presumably by stage coach—who'd receive it, edit it, and then publish it. Their stories back then followed the introduction-middle-conclusion students still use to write essays today: *It was a sunny morning as the president ate his breakfast. He went about his day, finishing up in a theater, where he was shot. He was rushed to a doctor who did this, that and the other, and then he died.*

But then the telegraph arrived. Reporters could transmit their story in hours rather than weeks, and today's news would feature in tomorrow's newspapers. The telegraph was faster, but it was unreliable for long messages. A twenty-word telegram made it through safely, but the reporters found their three hundred-word articles were often only partially transmitted before the line failed or you got kicked off the machine by a burly military type.

I asked, "Can you see what the problem with writing articles that way was?"

"If the conclusion, that the president died, is missing then the story loses its point. The story is only useful if it is transmitted in its entirety," Catherine said.

I nodded, waited a bit, and then gave them a nudge. "Can you see the connection between the way they structured their articles and how FPP is structured?"

Again it was Catherine who answered. "Their articles were valueless until they were transmitted in their entirety; FPP can't ship—which is when it becomes valuable—until all the testing is done. Is that what you mean?"

I nodded.

Tim looked down at his hands as if avoiding our eyes. "That's not strictly true, Catherine. Our current strategy is to deliver sooner by lowering quality."

"I think Craig and I have found a way to deliver sooner by increasing our quality. By building quality in," I replied.

I leaned forward and rested my arms on the table. "The reporters solved their problem by inverting their articles. Flipping them over so the most newsworthy paragraph, called the *lede* paragraph, was at the top, then next most important paragraph was next, and so on."

Gregor tilted his head. "So, even if their transmission was interrupted part way through, their editors still had a useful article?" He nodded to himself. "Very clever."

I let that sink in for a few moments. "I want us to invert FPP by delivering the most important paragraph first, then the next most important paragraph, and so on until we hit December 1st. Each paragraph—each small batch—must be good enough to ship."

Gregor frowned. "Good enough to ship?"

"Good enough to ship. We still won't ship until December 1st, but I want the code and the documentation and everything else for each small chunk fully tested, fully reworked and good enough quality that we could ship it, were it time."

Catherine didn't look happy. She waved her hand at the sticky-covered wall. "So, you're reneging on your promise you made at the end of the War Room. Is this just another way of descoping?"

"Yes, it is a severe descoping *now*, rather than later. By the time we leave this room, I hope to have pared the project back to just the three stickies we selected earlier. They'll make up our first chunk of good-enough-to-ship software. We will test and rework that small chunk until it is good enough to ship, and then we will start working on the next small chunk."

She shook her head. "But you can't tell me exactly what I'll get on December 1st?"

"Nope. But if we don't change, it's probable you'll get nothing."

"We will, using your analogy, have transmitted almost all of our article, but it won't be good enough to print?"

I nodded.

Her eyebrows furrowed. "Are you asking me for permission, Steve, or are you telling me this is how it's going to be?"

I looked around the table and made eye contact with each individual. "I'm saying this is how it has to be."

"In that case, we'd better decide what features go in this chunk, and then in the following ones," Catherine said.

Gregor said, "Phil, Tim and I can do that, as soon as we're finished here."

Catherine shook her head. "No. I need to be involved in that discussion too, Gregor."

He glanced at me; I shrugged. "Umm ...why?"

"I'm not getting every feature on the wall, right?"

Gregor looked at me.

I said, "It seems unlikely."

"In that case, I must prioritize the features to ensure we get the best possible product within the time available."

Gregor said, "You've already prioritized the stickies. I thought we'd tackle them in order."

She shook her head again. "That doesn't work for me. Let me show you." She went to the wall and grabbed one of the top three high-risk features, the one that needed CORETRAN work, and stuck it on the far right of the wall. "This is high risk, but it's far lower value than other features. I'd rather increase my odds of having the others and find a manual work-around for this one."

Catherine stepped away from the wall for a moment, then started rearranging the sticky notes. She crumpled up one sticky and replaced it with three others from different sides of the wall.

She turned back to me. "We've still got budget for this project until April 1st, right, Steve?"

"At least."

"So we can keep working this way, after we go live in December?"

Instinctively I agreed, though I hadn't actually thought that far ahead. "It's your budget."

"In that case," she said, picking up another bunch of sticky notes and moving them to the right a bit, "I don't need these until shortly after we go live."

"Great," I said, though I still felt nervous. We were sailing into uncharted territory, making this up as we went along.

The re-planning took another thirty minutes or so, and I sat back and watched as the team restructured the sticky notes on the wall. My only contribution was to ask *That would be good enough to ship, right?* every so often.

In the end we settled on a tiny chunk, the tip of the iceberg, that we figured would take between one and two weeks to finalize depending on what ugly issues we uncovered as we went.

Three weeks later, Phil's concerns about our messaging system having come true, we finally delivered our first chunk.

CHAPTER THIRTY-FIVE

And now there we were, all of us staring at the screen and waiting for the hourglass to disappear and for Catherine to verify that the numbers were all correct.

I glanced around the room. Everyone looked tense. There was a lot riding on this. The first chunk was almost good enough to ship, fully tested and reworked. All we needed to tip us from almost good enough to good enough was Catherine's confirmation that she was happy.

Finally, the cursor returned to its normal shape—it felt like minutes, but it could have only been seconds—and a small dialog box popped up, confirming that the customer's application form had been processed. Catherine clicked Okay, dismissing the dialog box, and swapped her "CSR" hat for one that said "CUSTOMER."

"Now, where's my confirmation letter?" she asked Tim.

Tim turned to Phil and nodded. Phil pressed a key on his laptop and the laser printer behind him hummed into life. Gregor had "borrowed" the printer from one of the production support teams. Fairness, as it should, came a distant second to survival.

Phil looked around the room. "This isn't a production environment, so I've redirected the confirmation letters to print here rather than through the mail center." He took the papers from the printer and passed them to Catherine, making a drum roll on his desk with his free hand.

Catherine compared the confirmation letter with her application form, then nodded her approval.

"Right. Now, show me the money."

Phil turned to Colin, another developer, who sat beside Catherine with a laptop open in front of him. Colin said, "This is exactly the same software you'd find in production, except it's not connected to the external banking system. Before I refresh the screen, can you check we haven't cheated and that the screen shows no payments for this customer?"

I pushed back in my chair and watched Catherine take control of the keyboard and check a few other things. She turned to me and said, with a serious tone to her voice, "Steven Abernethy, I am delighted with what I have seen. I've added a new basic-level customer, added their funds, set up their first application and seen the papers and payments come out. The functionality is, understandably, severely limited, but it does now contain our most important features."

I nodded to myself. In the last three weeks we'd identified just under three hundred and fifty defects and fixed every bug that kept the software from being judged good enough to ship. Many were caused by the underlying faults with the messaging system, and were only fixed after we flew three of the vendor's experts over from Australia.

Catherine smiled and looked around the room. "You know everyone, I was wondering if I'd ever see a real live system. How long ago did I sign off on the specifications for these screens? Was it nine months ago? Twelve?"

It was at least twelve months earlier, but we'd started creating those documents five months earlier.

Catherine continued. "I cannot tell you how good this feels, to finally get my hands on something concrete. I am so happy with everything I've seen and I'm really looking forward to seeing the next chunk."

"So is this chunk good enough to ship?" I asked.

She paused for a moment, then nodded. "You know, Steve. I do believe it is."

I thought I heard the room's old-fashioned windows rattle in their frames as everyone breathed out at once. The room came alive with mutual back-slapping.

"But," said Catherine, no longer smiling, "this chunk took three weeks, when we predicted it would take one or two. Sure, we crammed more features in than we expected while we fixed the messaging system. But that took us three weeks, and we have twelve remaining. That means we took twenty percent of our remaining duration to deliver ten percent of the scope. We need to double our speed, and then some, if we are going to make it. Can we speed up?"

I turned to Gregor. He turned to Tim. This was the testing phase, he was the testing manager. We'd agreed he should answer this question.

Tim stood. "That's a fair point." I detected a tinge of nervousness in his voice. "This first chunk was always going to be the most unpredictable and the slowest. We couldn't possibly know how long it would take to complete, so we guessed." He laughed awkwardly. "The next chunk will be hard work too, but I think we will soon be running a lot faster."

"You *think*?"

He frowned, then spoke slowly, as if he were giving complicated directions to a foreign tourist. "I say think, Catherine, because I can't prove it. In the last three weeks we've fixed a lot of serious underlying problems which now we won't have to fix again. And we've been learning to work in this new way. The first few attempts when you learn to ride a bike are always wobbly. We will speed up."

Catherine bit her lip before speaking. "But ... you can't guarantee we will have delivered a commercially viable product by December?"

Tim looked at Gregor, then sat, handing him the baton.

"Will we increase our speed enough so that the percentage of scope delivered equals the percentage of time elapsed?" He shrugged. "I honestly don't know. In another week, we'll know more. A week after that, we'll know even more ..."

"Okay," said Catherine, looking sad. "Can you track those two percentages, over time? Put them on a chart, so everyone can see?"

He said he would be glad to do that.

I said, "Thank you, everyone, for your hard work," and the room slowly emptied.

When just Catherine and I remained, she said, "You know, I just wish a month had already passed and we had a better idea of how fast we could run."

"I know."

I wished that Craig, who had inspired this situation, could have joined in, but he was still on vacation.

Friday, September 22nd
FPP launch date - December 1st, this year

CHAPTER THIRTY-SIX

"The Queen thinks the world smells of wet paint, Steven."

Erm. I glanced down at Eleanor, trying to figure out what she meant.

She'd just stepped out of the lift and I had expected her to castigate me, maybe even castrate me, but instead she chose to complicate things by sharing bewildering facts about the British royal family.

"According to my husband, she does." Perhaps it was an accountant joke?

She smiled to herself, gestured around the sixth floor, and whispered, "Look at how magnificently busy everyone is."

I'd passed the word around that everyone better be well-dressed and on their best behavior for Eleanor's visit, given what happened last time she visited our floor. We'd not painted anything, but we had tidied the place up a good bit. I knew Eleanor was going to beat me up later that morning, so I was keen to make the best impression I could before then.

I smiled and decided to tell Eleanor my own royal family joke. I made it up when I was twelve. "And I heard that the Queen wears three hundred-pound knickers. She must weigh a ton when she's fully dressed."

I smiled.

Eleanor didn't.

"I have no idea what you are talking about, Steven. Now, where is this demonstration taking place?"

We were about to demonstrate our third chunk of potentially shippable software to Eleanor. Ten days had passed since we had finally demonstrated the first, four days since our second. Catherine had invited Mark Richmond to the second demo, and Eleanor invited herself to view the third.

I pointed across the room to the conference room. "My team is looking forward to seeing you again. We've catered a buffet lunch, and we'll demonstrate the software as we eat."

"The *GETS* software?" she asked, emphasizing the word GETS, which she'd decided was easier to say than "Good Enough To Ship." It had caught on throughout the company. I'd met with her a half dozen times during the previous weeks, bringing her up to speed with our new approach, and she genuinely seemed to like it.

"Absolutely."

"And FPP is currently technically, but not commercially, GETS. Correct?"

"Correct." Not enough of the overall system was good enough to ship yet, though more and more bits were being tested and fixed every day, so we were getting there.

"Do you and your project manager have a date for when the system will be commercially GETS?"

"Not yet."

She paused and crossed her arms, but kept her face neutral. "Will everyone fit in your tiny conference room, Steven?"

"They will. They're there already, waiting for us. All except for Craig Lally." I checked my watch. "He'll be joining us in a few minutes. And then he's flying off to Norway, later in the day."

I was leaving work early too. The kids and I were flying to Euro Disney for the weekend. I hadn't been around much in recent months and I owed them something special. They didn't know about it, but I'd been dropping hints.

"Your *small* conference room?" She looked across at the room and then her frown deepened. "Oh, Steven. I wanted to meet your *entire* team, not just your leadership team."

She scanned the floor, then charged off across the room. I followed along behind, no idea where she was heading. She stopped abruptly in front of a bank of desks where three of my staff sat: a skinny young Polish guy called Krzysztof who worked as an analyst; Brian, a beefy Northern Irish developer who had a reputation for being quietly competent; and Sharon, one of our younger testers who started working in our call centers fresh out of school before making her way into our IT department. Shortly after inverting FPP, Tim and Gregor had re-organized the teams into several smaller teams. Each team included at least one person from each role, and they all sat together to work on a specific feature. I didn't know what feature this small team worked on. I hoped my ignorance wouldn't matter.

Eleanor eyed Krzysztof, Brian, and Sharon for a moment. She looked like a hungry lioness picking out an antelope for dinner. Using her finely tuned hunting instincts, she picked Krzysztof—clearly the skinniest and weakest antelope.

She stuck out her hand and said cheerfully, "Hello, I'm Eleanor Scharlau. I'm the Chief Financial Officer. Tell me, who are you, young man?"

Krzysztof looked startled. I felt terrified. Kryz was an excellent technician, but he wasn't big on political smarts. I hoped he wouldn't embarrass himself. No, that's not quite true. I wasn't all that bothered if he embarrassed himself; I just hoped he didn't embarrass me.

"This is Krzysztof," I said quietly, trying to hide my frustration that Eleanor had so blatantly disrupted and taken control of my well-planned morning.

She turned and glared. "I'm quite sure Krzysztof knows his own name, Steven," then turned back to Kryz and smiled in a way that could be described as charming—if you didn't know better.

She smiled widely at Kryz, like the politician she was, then reached out and gently touched him on his lower arm. "How are things going?"

I scanned the room and identified the emergency exits.

Kryz asked, eyes darting to me, if she was referring to life in general or FPP in particular.

Eleanor chuckled. "Why don't you tell me about both?"

Kryz said that generally, he was doing fine, thank you very much for asking. He paused as he chose his next words carefully. "Eleanor, the first thing about FPP that is good is how it does not feel anymore like we are flogging a dead horse." Eleanor told him that was nice. He continued. "The second thing is that I was not pleased at all when Steve announced FPP was starting the testing phase early. I am an analyst, not a tester, so I hate testing. You see?"

Eleanor *tsked*, then leaned in towards him and said just loud enough that only Kryz and I could hear, "But isn't it common practice, Kryz, for analysts to help out with the testing? I'm sure Steve explained that to me once."

"It is. And, some analysts don't mind doing monkey work. But I do."

I cringed. Many of my analysts, and developers too, disliked doing testing—especially long runs of it. Testing is a specific skill; it requires a different temperament and a different (some say evil) way of thinking. I understood that they didn't like it, but there wasn't always enough analysis work during the testing phase to keep the analysts busy. However, there was always more than enough testing for them to do. They grumbled, but had more sense than to call it monkey work in front of our CFO. Most of them, anyway.

At least, I thought, Kryz hadn't made actual monkey noises.

Eleanor pulled a sad face, then glared at me. "Oh. That's a shame."

I shrugged. What did she expect? If she'd only wanted to hear good news then she should have stuck to my carefully choreographed good news tour.

Kryz said, "But anyway, that doesn't matter so much now. FPP, like we're doing it now, is different than other projects I've worked on. It is not perfect, but it is different. And better. Don't get me wrong, the first chunk was horrible, very stressful and loads of testing and waiting and more testing. *Boring.* The second chunk was a little less stressful, less monkey work, less downtime. And this last chunk is even a bit better. I do some testing each week and I also do some analysis. A bit of testing, a bit of analysis. A bit more testing, a bit more analysis. And you know what? The three of us have gotten pretty good at doing the testing, analysis and rework together. This is the first time since I've been working here that analysts, developers and testers have worked together as a team." He nodded emphatically. "I like that very much."

Eleanor started to speak, but Kryz had more to say.

"What's best, though, is that when I look forward from here, I see that every week or so we will actually finish something. We finish something and then we give it to our customers and they tell us whether they like it or not. That is good, actually."

Eleanor nodded and told Kryz that Catherine and her team were very pleased with how things were going. They'd be even happier, she added, if they knew for sure we'd deliver on December 1st.

"Catherine is a very nice lady." Kryz smiled. "She told us that starting our new Inverted Pyramid way of working had been like force-feeding our department a pile of prunes. We finally got things flowing."

Eleanor smiled, then invited herself into the cubicle. I followed her in, still not sure how this was all going to end.

Eleanor asked Kryz to show her what he was currently working on. We sat, and Eleanor pointed at a silver framed photograph that sat amongst several piles of paper, a collection a miniature themed chess sets and two deadish-looking cacti. Eleanor asked if the picture was of his girlfriend. He said it was his in fact his fiancée, and they discussed his wedding plans for a very long five minutes. Kryz invited Eleanor to attend his wedding, but unfortunately, it turned out that Eleanor was in Barcelona the weekend of Kryz's wedding, otherwise she would have loved to attend. She said.

At last, Eleanor asked Kryz what was on his screen. He said that he and Sharon were both regression testing part of the system. Eleanor asked if he thought the software was good enough to ship. He said that provided their coming round of regression testing proved they hadn't broken anything while fixing the newly found bugs, then it would be. So far they'd found no new problems.

He told her she could drive for a while and passed her the mouse. He showed her where to click on the screen and then guided her smoothly through the many screens of the new FPP application. I presume Kryz deliberately guided her away from the parts of the system that weren't yet GETS, because there were no disasters.

As they played around with the software, I looked across the floor towards the conference room where FPP's leadership team waited. Phil and Vrinda stood at the window watching us. Phil held his arm out in front of him and tapped his watch, then rubbed his stomach in exaggerated circular movements. I made a face back at them and decided to let Eleanor continue on with her demo. This was the first time she'd ever seen, up close and personal, the software we were working on. In some ways, this was better than the stage-managed demo waiting for her in the conference room. It was scarier, but also more believable, more concrete. And if we *were* genuinely shipping GETS software, Eleanor shouldn't stumble across too many problems.

A few minutes into Kryz's tour, I felt a light tap on my arm. I turned to see Craig Lally standing beside me with a friendly grin on his face. His beard was a good inch longer than the last time I had seen him and his face was tanned.

I shook his hand, whispered, "Hi ya," then pointed at Eleanor and did a thumbs-up gesture.

He mouthed, "Good."

I decided to give Eleanor and Kryz just another minute. The sausage rolls would have cooled by now, and the sandwiches would be warm. And we were way behind schedule.

I whispered to Craig, "Good trip?"

"Yep."

I cleared my throat to get their attention. Eleanor and the others turned to face me. Eleanor acknowledged Craig with a smile and I said, "We really should wrap things up."

Eleanor agreed and put down the mouse, but before she could stand, Kryz asked her if she wanted to see something *really* interesting.

"Really interesting?"

He nodded. "We have figured out a very cheap, simple way to find bugs in the software without actually testing it."

She glanced at me, then turned back to Kryz and said, "Of course, Kryz. I'm always interested in really interesting things."

CHAPTER THIRTY-SEVEN

Kryz moved one of the dead cacti from atop the pile of books, folders and papers it protected and placed it to one side. He rifled through the pile and pulled an inch-thick ring binder from near the bottom and held it up for us all to see. I recognized from the cover that it was onc of FPP's specification documents. He flipped through the pages then laid the document open on the table so that Eleanor and I could see it. He said it was the original specification for the screens he had just shown Eleanor.

"This was one of the first features we tested, in the first chunk. We've just been regression testing it, to check it still works, since we sometimes accidentally break software when adding something new." He paused to check that Eleanor was paying full attention. "Now, Eleanor, I must inform you, lest you think I am incompetent, that I spent many hours preparing this specification many, many months ago, and it was reviewed several times and all the right people signed off on it before Brian here built it. You understand?"

"Are you telling me this, Kryz, so that when I see something not-so-good I will know you did a good job?"

"I am. Despite all the effort we put into writing accurate requirements documents, they still contained a lot of ambiguous requirements, which result in us finding defects which then needed to be reworked. Okay?"

She nodded. "Of course."

"Before I explain what we used to do, and what we now do, I need to explain some background. When we started delivering GETS software, Gregor made us all move desks so that we sat in small, focused test-and-rework teams. He said he wanted to get rid of the piles of half-done work that build up between teams that sit separately. Brian, Sharon and I, we are a team and we now sit together. Previously, Sharon and all the testers worked on the fourth floor, and Brian and I sat with our own analyst and developer teams, placed at different ends of the sixth floor. It was this sitting together that enabled us to discover our way of finding defects without testing."

He paused, as if collecting his thoughts. "We made our discovery a few weeks ago, during the first chunk. Sharon has just finished testing this particular specification." He pointed at the page he had unearthed for us. "And guess what, Eleanor?"

Eleanor shook her head. "I've no idea, Kryz. Tell me."

"She found defects! I told you that already, Eleanor."

Eleanor's face blanked and she glared at me, annoyed that I'd wasted her time. I shrugged my shoulders. She should have stuck to the script. I glanced at Craig and made what I hoped looked like an apologetic smile. He smiled back as if to say that he didn't mind.

Seemingly oblivious, Kryz continued with his story. "In fact, she found lots of defects! But that's okay because that's why we test things."

Eleanor smiled, but it looked to me like the thin veneer of charm she'd painted on her face was about to crack.

Kryz smiled back. "Now, normally, Sharon would just log the defects into her defect tracking software so that Brian could fix them later, and then she'd carry on doing more testing. But, for some reason, perhaps it was because we were sitting next to each other, Sharon did something very unusual. She spun around in her chair and tapped us both on our shoulders. Well, she actually tapped me on the shoulder, and then Brian, and then the three of us had a good chat about these bugs she had just found.

"This is when we made our really interesting discovery. After a bit of chat, we realized we could have found many of these bugs without Sharon *actually* doing any testing. And that's what we do now. We three talk about how we expect the software to behave, before we test it, and if we disagree on how we think the software should behave then that means the requirements I wrote were probably ambiguous and Brian has probably built something different than what I intended."

I was suddenly intrigued as I sensed, at last, the direction he was headed. "Ambiguous requirements, Kryz?"

"Yes," his eyes grew wide. "I asked for X, Brian interpreted X differently than what I intended and wrote software that did Y. It is very common. The English language is sometimes open to many interpretations."

Eleanor shook her head. "This doesn't make any sense."

I explained that ambiguous and vague specifications were very common causes of rework in software projects all around the world, and that was why—as Kryz had gone to pains to describe—we spent so much time trying to get our specs right up front.

"A lot of good that did you." She turned to Kryz. "Can you give me an example of ambiguous requirements?"

He thought a moment then grinned. "When I started working here, Phil, who is one of our senior programmers and who likes his coffee very much, suggested I try the coffee from a little Italian cafe he likes just off High Street. So I did, and he was right, so I emailed him and said thank you for his recommendation. He emailed me back and said, 'Good. Once you try their coffee, you'll never go back.' Which surprised me because I intended on going back."

Eleanor said nothing for a moment, then snarfed (snorted and laughed at the same time), something I've never heard her do before, nor thankfully, since. She said, "I guess, this time, it was my request to you that was ambiguous. I meant an example of a defect that was caused by ambiguous requirements."

Kryz said, "Of course." He picked up a sheaf of papers from his desk and flipped through the pages so we could all see. The pages were covered in red circles, maybe two or three per page. "This was something we worked on yesterday. Every red circle is a potential defect we found when Brian, Sharon and I disagreed about how we expected the software to behave."

He pointed at the first circle. "You see this one? It requires that under certain circumstances, the system must pay a refund into the customer's bank account. Seems simple, right? The problem is, the customer might have more than one bank account set up on our system, and although I didn't write it explicitly, I meant that the refund should be into the account the original payment came from. When Brian wrote the code, he assumed the refund should go to the customer's default account. You understand?"

We nodded.

"It was only yesterday, when we listed out the scenarios we should test to prove that the requirement was fulfilled, that we realized it wasn't absolutely clear how the software was supposed to behave. We raised a bug, and this morning Catherine's team decided the code needs to be changed, which Brian will do today. Then, either today or tomorrow, Sharon or I will test not only that this scenario works but also that we've not inadvertently broken anything while fixing it."

Eleanor said, "I understand now. So you find this type of defect sooner, by talking and testing that you have a shared understanding, before you test the actual software. If you disagree about how the software should behave, then you probably have a defect which then needs to be fixed."

"That is correct, Eleanor."

"It's an awful shame, Kryz, that you didn't have those conversations a long time ago, before the software was built.

He nodded emphatically. "This project could have prevented a lot of defects and avoided a lot of rework."

Kryz described the next three circled defects before Eleanor put her hand up to stop him. "I need a moment to think this through. Please." She looked down at the floor and closed her eyes.

I mouthed "well done!" to Kryz and Sharon and Brian, but my pleasure was brief. A few moments later, Eleanor opened her eyes and turned to me—though turned *on* me might be a better way of putting it. I flinched when I saw her face. Her jaw was tight and her eyes had narrowed in anger.

"What I simply do not understand," she barked at me, "is why you did not have these conversations months ago, before you built the software!"

I stepped back involuntarily. "Pardon?"

"How much rework could you have prevented if you'd prevented the defects in the first place?"

"I don't know, I ..."

"Maybe you could have delivered FPP by now."

"I don't ... perhaps ..."

"Steven. Right now most of your staff are either fixing or retesting defects. If only your teams had collaborated and challenged the requirements before building the software, we'd have surely shipped FPP now."

I shook my head. "Maybe ..."

She ignored me and turned to Craig. "You manufacturing folk wouldn't ever build something without clearly specifying how to test it first, would you?"

He thought a moment before answering. "We always specify tolerances as part of specifications. You know: 'the widget has to be ten mm long plus or minus five thousandths of a mm.' How else would we set up our machines? How else would we procure our raw materials? How would we test the widgets after we'd created them?"

Eleanor, her face now completely devoid of charm, said, "Of course you do. That's one of the ways you build quality in to your processes. Good carpenters measure twice and cut once too." She turned to me. "And Steven, I imagine that even you techies specify how you'd like your steak done when you order it, rather than after it's cooked. Correct?"

"Of course we do. But—"

"But nothing. It is clear to me FPP has been delayed considerably because your team is now busy fixing these requirements defects, many of which could have been avoided. Why is that? Why didn't your analysts, developers and testers have these conversations earlier?"

I shook my head as I struggled to find an answer. "Honestly, best practice is to keep developers and testers separate. That way, testers find more defects."

"Is that true, Sharon?"

Sharon glanced at me then Eleanor, looking nervous that she'd just found herself stuck in the middle of an argument between her boss's boss's boss and her boss's boss's boss's boss.

"When we work independently, we come to the software with fresh eyes and we do tend to find more bugs."

"But that's after the software has been built? Correct?"

"Yes."

"Wouldn't you be better off using your fresh eyes to prevent defects rather than finding them?"

Sharon nodded cautiously. "Though we still couldn't prevent all defects—maybe only half of them."

Eleanor nodded assertively, as if the case had been closed. She turned to Kryz. "Have you shared your new way of working with anyone else?"

He said, "Not yet."

Eleanor turned back to me. "Did you know about this team's innovation before now?"

I felt my neck redden. "We've been busy ramping up ..."

"So I've just been doing your job for you. Great. Have any of your other teams come up with good ideas we should know about?"

I hung my head. "I don't know."

And then my public interrogation and humiliation suddenly stopped. Her arms flopped by her sides and she looked down at the ground. She muttered, "What an embarrassment," then she looked up and said, "I suppose we should get to your little demonstration then."

I said, "Yes."

She thanked Kryz, Sharon and Brian once more, carefully shaking each of their hands, and then she, Craig and I made our way in silence to the conference room.

When we reached the conference room door, Eleanor stopped. "I don't need to see your demonstration. I want you to dismiss everyone and then I will talk with just you and Gregor."

"Dismiss?" I said, worried by both her choice of words and her instruction.

"That's what I said." She looked at Craig. "I'm so sorry Craig, I meant to thank you properly for all the good work you've done for us, but I need to talk to Steve and Gregor in private.

Craig tipped his head and said he understood. He shook both our hands and left.

"Eleanor," I said as I shook my head, indignant. "This demonstration is not just for your benefit. This team has worked hard on this and I need you to acknowledge that and to say a few words of thanks."

"Tough."

CHAPTER THIRTY-EIGHT

Eleanor slammed her fist down on the table. "Will you two deliver FPP on December 1st? Yes or No?"

It was just Gregor, Eleanor and me in the room.

Eleanor sat at the head of the table, ready to carve the two of us up.

I glanced at Gregor, half hoping he'd answer and take the heat off me. He looked down at his hands and said nothing, which was precisely what he should have done.

I said, "We might. We don't know yet."

"What does that mean? Does it mean you have a plan which shows there's a possibility you will deliver? Or does it mean you do not even have a plan, so you really and truly are clueless? Which is it?"

I let out a long breath. "It's the second option. We don't have a plan yet."

"You're clueless?"

I nodded, then hung my head.

"Do you know how much is riding on this product?"

Before I could answer, and probably make things worse, Gregor looked up and said, "We've been very busy, Eleanor, getting the project back on track."

"I understand that, Gregor," she snapped. "I've just spent some quality time with one of your teams, and it's clear you are transforming your project. I am impressed, and under different ... circumstances, I'd be delighted."

I thought I noticed her chin quiver as she spoke.

I leaned forward and quietly asked, "Circumstances?"

She closed her eyes and rubbed them with the backs of her hands. A few moments passed, then she spoke to me quietly and deliberately. "Halifax and I have made a very big promise to some very important people. We cannot keep our promise unless real customers are buying FPP on December 1st."

I nodded but said nothing, hoping she would share more.

She looked at Gregor, then back at me and said, "Was it not obvious when Halifax declared that we would ship on December 1st and beat Chaste to market that it was an act of desperation?"

Her face had turned ashen. When Hal burned our boats, it was not just bravado. He'd made a big bet that we would deliver on time and he would, therefore, keep his promise. Or else.

I looked at Gregor. "We can have a plan together by ... Friday?"

He nodded emphatically. "Friday."

"And will this plan tell me whether we can definitely launch by December 1st or not?"

Gregor and I both said, "Yes."

"I need it by Monday."

I glanced at Gregor. He nodded.

I said, "Monday evening."

She nodded. "Right. Now, let me be clear. If there's a plausible risk we won't be live on December 1st, then I need to know. Do you understand?"

"Yes."

Gregor looked directly at Eleanor, "Can you tell us more about the promise you have made?"

"I could, but I most certainly will not."

"Can you tell us what the consequences are if we're not live on December 1st?"

Her mouth tightened. "Jobs are at stake, and not just Hal's and mine."

She stood and headed to the door, then turned back towards us. "Just in case it's not utterly clear, I will be delighted if you come back to me on Monday with an honest and emphatic *yes*, but I will be enormously unhappy and vindictive if you tell me *yes* and then we run late. Do you both understand that?"

We both nodded like two schoolboys relieved they'd not been expelled. "Yes."

She stepped out of the meeting room and gently closed the door behind her.

As soon as the door was shut, Gregor pushed himself back in his chair. "There goes our weekends."

"Sorry about that."

He shrugged. "It's part of the job. I wasn't doing much, anyway."

I said, "I'm booked to take my kids to Euro Disney this weekend. It was meant to be a surprise."

"That's a pity." He frowned, then offered a half-hearted smile. "Though, I guess, it's lucky your kids don't know what they're missing out on."

"What makes you think it was luck?" I said, grimacing. "I stopped making promises to my kids a long time ago. It wasn't fair."

We spent the next quarter of an hour figuring out how to produce our plan. To be fair, it was something we would have started shortly, whether we'd talked to Eleanor or not. Gregor already had the bare minimum list of test scenarios that had to pass before we could go live, as well as estimates for how long it would take to execute them. We didn't know how many defects we would find or how long it would take to fix and then retest them, but we could estimate those. Given those inputs, we knew we could come up with best, most likely, and worst case delivery dates.

Gregor said, "You know, Steve, if we come back with a maybe, and I think we will, then Eleanor's going to be very unhappy."

"I got that impression."

"But there is another option open to us. A get-out-of-jail free option. Except it's not free, of course, nothing is."

"Is there?"

"We could easily slip back to plan A—lower our quality standards and stop producing GETS software. Then we'll hit our date, no problem. We can fix the problems after we go live. Hardly anyone will buy the product until April, anyway."

I shook my head. I really did not want to do that. But, as a last resort . . .

Sunday, September 24th
FPP launch date - December 1st, this year

CHAPTER THIRTY-NINE

"You look like a bag of bums, Steven."

It was 4:52 p.m., Sunday. I was standing in our little kitchen with Mom. I'd spent all weekend working with Gregor, and I was exhausted and sick of him and his spreadsheets. And now, apparently, I didn't look my best.

"Thanks, Mom," I said. "We have ten weeks to go. We're already one-third of the way through our recovery, but we've only delivered one-sixth of our minimum set of features. We have sped up, but even so we cannot make December 1st."

"But you've put so much work into this project."

"Yeah." It was kind of her to say, but it didn't help.

I watched as she put the kids' dinner, little smiley face pizzas, onto a baking tray. The girls would have helped prepare them earlier. She slid them in the oven, then we went through to the lounge and sat.

One of our cats—the girls named him Perronimo, but we just called him Mo—came in and meowed for attention. I crouched down and rubbed him on the back of the neck.

"If we get incredibly lucky, we'll deliver a bare bones system in late November. More likely, we'll deliver sometime in February or March. If things go badly ... well ..."

"How often do you get incredibly lucky, Steve?"

"Never. We know we'll speed up, but we'd have to run at least twice as fast as we've assumed to have a reasonable chance of hitting December 1st."

She said, "Oh dear." I went to the oven and checked the pizzas through the glass window. The cheese hadn't quite started bubbling yet, but they looked good. How come the girls were allowed pizza for their dinner and I wasn't?

"They need a couple more minutes."

"I know," Mom said. "Now tell me. What did Craig say about all this?"

I looked down and mumbled, "I haven't spoken to him."

"Speak up, Steven. It sounded like you said you hadn't spoken to him."

I looked up at her. "He's traveling. I haven't spoken to him."

"He's got a phone, hasn't he?"

I shrugged teenager-like, using just one shoulder, and grunted, "S'pose."

"Steven," she said disapprovingly. She went to the door and called the children.

Much later, my darling mother would describe this as the moment when the impossible happened: A man stopped, admitted he was lost and asked for directions for the second time in the same calendar year. I called Craig.

My call went straight to voice mail. I listened to his message but hung up before the beep.

I shouted so Mom could hear me, "Voicemail. He's in Latvia." Oh well, at least I tried.

"So email him."

"Okay. Later."

She came to the door. "Do it now. And since you've been such a good boy, you can have some of the kids' pizza."

I made a sulky face and pulled out my phone. I tapped out a quick email summarizing my situation and asking Craig for his advice.

The kids came in, and we sat around the table and talked while we ate. School was good. TV was better. Boys were smelly. Alison thought pink was the best color in the world; Ashley, being older and wiser, thought it was babyish. Those sorts of things. Important things.

Then we played a game called "Jump on Dad," which involved me lying down on their trampoline, pretending to be asleep, and them jumping on me with a *splat.* If they jumped hard enough then they woke me up and I had to chase them, kiss them, and tickle them until I got so tired I fell asleep again. After ten minutes of that I took them upstairs and gave them a bath.

When I finally made it back downstairs Mom said she'd heard my phone beep.

Craig had emailed me.

Where is FPP's bottleneck?

I read his response out loud.

Mom asked, "Where is it?"

"I don't know."

"Then email him back and tell him you don't know."

I did as I was told.

He responded ten minutes later.

Look, so far you've turned your software development teams into a factory—a test-scenario processing factory. You need to figure out where your bottleneck is because it determines how fast your factory runs.
I want you to read *The Goal* and follow its instructions. You'll find a copy in my office. Cheryl may still have a copy too.
I'm off scuba diving very early tomorrow morning and then I'm out of email/phone range for the following three days, canyoning. I don't know what canyoning is, but I had to sign a half dozen waiver forms because of my age. Wish me luck!

A moment later, another email beeped for attention.

Ask Cheryl to show you her bottleneck.

I read the emails to Mom, and then downloaded the ebook version of *The Goal* to my tablet. Two minutes later, I sat on my office couch reading it. It was a full-length novel, not a text book, so I couldn't just flip to the index and look up "bottleneck." I hunkered down.

Forty minutes later, Mom called me to my dinner. I wolfed it down, then when I revealed I was only on page thirty-two, mom said she'd do the clean-up—just this once!—provided I bought the audiobook version and listened to it on double-speed.

I did as I was told. And soon I was sound asleep on my couch with the book playing away in the background.

I woke just after 1:30 a.m. I was still on the couch but someone—a burglar perhaps? Maybe my Mom?—had removed my glasses, unplugged my earphones and placed a blanket over me. I dragged myself upstairs to bed and set my alarm for extra early.

Monday, September 25th FPP launch date - December 1st, this year

CHAPTER FORTY

"You're not one of them vegetarians, are you?"

The clock on Cheryl's office wall said it was 6:17 a.m.

"Nope."

She said in that case, she'd be delighted to tell me about the book and—even better—her bottlenecks. But first, she insisted on cooking me up a bacon and egg breakfast.

"Bacon and eggs?"

"That's what I said."

"Love some."

I yawned my thanks, and a few minutes later she returned with a large plate and an extra-large mug filled with thick black coffee. Lavazza, she said, Pavarotti's favorite. She plucked a mandarin from the fruit bowl on her desk and peeled it while I tucked into my breakfast.

"So this book, *The Goal*. It's a novel, a business novel. It's about this factory manager, called Alex, who rescues his factory from closure by cutting his batch sizes and managing his bottleneck, among other things."

I munched away on my breakfast while she talked.

"First, you know what a real bottleneck is, right? It's the neck of the bottle. The skinniest part at the top. What would happen if you went out into the dining area, grabbed one of those big water cooler bottles out there and upended it?

"Water would rush out."

"How long would it take to empty the bottle? Guess."

I imagined lifting the bottle, hefting it upside down and watching the water pour out: *glug, glug, glug.* "A minute?"

"And what if the bottle's neck were skinnier?"

"It would take longer."

"And if it were wider?

"It would flow faster."

She nodded. "That's the thing with bottlenecks. They're only a tiny part of the bottle, but they determine how fast stuff flows. With me?"

"Yes."

"More coffee?"

"Not yet."

"Before I tell you about our bottleneck, let me tell you about the person who taught me about bottlenecks.

"Soon after Craig visited, we got so busy with new customers we couldn't keep up. You could say our success was a disaster. I called Craig, and he asked me where my bottleneck was. I said I didn't know, and he sent me to meet Mahjella, who works in the accounts department of the Wyx-Fin Bank."

Sounded familiar. "Did she cook you breakfast?"

Cheryl ignored my question. "Mahjella ran Wyx-Bank's accounts payable team. They pay the bank's suppliers' invoices. Apparently, everything was going dandy until they got a new computer system that had a few problems and left them with a big backlog of unpaid invoices. Basically, they couldn't keep up with their work.

"Mahjella told me how they processed each invoice following five steps. First, someone opened the mail and checked the invoice. Second, someone matched the invoice up with a purchase order. Third, they keyed the details into the computer. Fourth, they assigned an accounting code and approved the payment. And, fifth, they pushed a button on the computer which submitted a whole batch of invoices to be paid."

She put the mandarin down and held up her left hand, fingers fanned out.

"Now, a question for you." She pointed to the thumb on her left hand. "Let's say this thumb represents step one, and they could open a hundred invoices each hour." She moved to the index finger, then across the other fingers one at a time. "They can do eighty invoices an hour in step two, one-twenty in step three, fifty in the fourth step, and the little pinkie, a computerized batch process, processed thousands in a matter of minutes. Given those numbers, what's the most they can process in an hour, Steve?"

I pointed to her fourth finger. "Fifty."

She nodded. "That's the bottleneck. If you needed to process more invoices, where would you focus your efforts?"

"That fourth step. Figure out how to do sixty units per hour and the entire team's output would jump up by twenty percent."

She smiled slyly. "If they made any other step faster, would the department process any more invoices?"

"No."

"Exactly!" She slapped her hand on the table for effect. "Mahjella had twelve people in her team, but she was the only person authorized to do the bottleneck process. The others worked on steps one through three."

I thought a moment, then said, "Was she the bottleneck? The point to improve?"

Cheryl picked up the mandarin again and nodded. "And guess what? She didn't spend all of her time doing step four, because she spent much of her day on the phone apologizing to suppliers who wanted their invoices paid."

"She was a busy lady."

"Aren't we all ..." Cheryl shook her head. "But anyway. Once Mahjella realized she was the bottleneck, it took her less than an hour to figure out how to sort things out. Can you guess what she did?"

I finished off the last bite of my bacon and eggs, then took a slurp of coffee.

"She had to stop talking to suppliers, so I bet she locked herself away in a room somewhere and just focused on step four."

"Bingo! She did some other things too. Her senior staff started checking every invoice before it reached her, so she didn't waste her precious bottleneck time working on bad data. Her team started opening the mail first thing each morning so Mahjella was never starved of work. Within a week, she said, they'd cleared their backlog, the unhappy phone calls went away, and everything was all hunky-dory."

Cheryl finished her mandarin and picked up another, peeling it and passing me a couple of segments. "We all know the secret to life is focus. But that only works if you know where to focus: your bottleneck."

I bit down and the mandarin's sweet juices flooded inside my mouth.

"Where was your bottleneck, Cheryl?"

"We didn't have one."

"Oh." I wasn't sure how to respond. Then I saw her lips curled into a smile. She was teasing me. "Before Craig helped us, we didn't have a bottleneck because we had far more capacity than we did customers. It was only after we fixed our quality problems and more staff started coming downstairs for lunch, rather than going to High Street, that all my spare capacity got used up. One week we were fine, the next we were unusually busy, the next we had long queues out in the serving area and folk started to complain. From good to bad, like fresh fish on a hot day.

"I spoke to Mahjella, then I read *The Goal* and went looking for my bottleneck. When I found it, it was obvious—in hindsight."

"So where was it?"

"China."

"Where?"

"Not where. *What.* Follow me."

She picked up my plate, empty if you ignored the streaks of egg yolk, and led me out through the kitchen to the swinging doors. She opened them and then turned back to face the kitchen. I did the same.

"I spent hours wandering around inside the kitchen, trying to spot clues that would point to my bottleneck, but nothing jumped out at me. No piles of unfinished work, like in the book, no abnormal screaming or shouting."

She led me into the serving area. "But when I watched our customers lining up and waiting to be served, the bottleneck jumped out at me. See down there. The china."

She pointed at two tall stacks of plates sitting behind the serving area. "We didn't have enough clean plates during peak hours to serve all our new customers."

"Did you call this your "China Syndrome" by chance?"

"Nope," she said, smiling patiently. "Now, imagine it's 12:30, peak time, and suddenly the customers stop moving and the queue starts to build up. And why's that? There's plenty of food, plenty of serving staff, but no plates. I ask the servers, *Where're all the damned plates?* and they say they've run out. I ask what they've done about it, and they say they've told the dishwashers and they're expecting a fresh batch through in a few minutes. And true enough, within minutes clean plates arrive and we start serving again. But not before a queue has built up and we'd lost a few impatient customers to High Street."

I smiled, knowing what came next. "So you bought more plates?"

She shook her head, her jaw set firmly. "Nope. I couldn't ask for more money, so I did what it said to do in the book. Before spending lots of money, try to make your bottleneck more efficient." She shrugged. "It turned out, we had plenty of plates; the trouble was that most of them were ..."

I realized I was meant to finish her sentence. "Dirty?"

She nodded. "Follow me." She led me through the kitchen to the dishwashing area and placed my breakfast plate on a rack that sat on a small conveyor belt in front of a silver machine. "This is our dishwasher."

I nodded, though it didn't look like any dishwasher I'd seen before.

"Watch this." She pushed a button and the conveyor started moving, carrying my dirty plate through the machine.

"It takes eight seconds for a dirty plate to travel through the washer, and the water is so hot, it's evaporated and the plates are dry when they come out the other side." She picked up my plate and added it to a stack of clean plates.

"Our bottleneck was caused because our dishwashers worked in big batches. We had plenty of plates, but too many were sitting waiting to be cleaned or waiting to be moved back to their serving area. We switched to smaller batches, kept the plates circulating, and the bottleneck went away."

We went back to her office. "The thing about bottlenecks is that once you get rid of one, another eventually takes its place. It's like playing Whack-A-Mole. Our next bottleneck was at the tills. We had enough money by then, so we purchased another till and employed a part-time cashier.

"These days I have spare capacity, so I don't have a bottleneck. As we keep growing, our next bottleneck will be the number of seats in our dining area. I'm trying to avoid that by adding more takeout options and I'm considering a delivery service."

I thanked Cheryl for her time, her food for thought and her

food for real.

She offered me one parting thought. "We used to be a disliked cost center, you know. Nowadays we are a much-liked profit center. It's a much happier place to work, what with the happy customers and happy bosses."

It was still early, and it was a beautiful morning. It felt wrong to waste it sitting at a desk. I called Phil, figuring he'd be running or cycling into work.

He answered quickly. "What's up, dude?"

I asked him to meet me atop Lord Kelvin's Peak, ASAP.

CHAPTER FORTY-ONE

Kelvin Park sits in the middle of Watt's Bridge City, occupying twenty acres of prime real estate all protected by royal decree. Kelvin's Peak, an extinct volcanic cone named after Lord Kelvin, the great scientist who laid the first transatlantic telegraph cable, among other things, sits in the middle of the park. It was quiet when I reached the peak, but it would soon fill up with tourists and school kids, and in the early afternoon, office workers taking exercise and lunch.

I carried two cups of takeout coffee with me, and I settled on a park bench and sipped mine while I waited for Phil.

I tried to figure out where our bottleneck was. Craig, in his email, described our project as a "test-processing factory," which was a fair description of any project in its testing phase. Our testers transformed our specifications into test scenarios, which they then executed. Developers fixed failing tests, which were retested. When all of the test scenarios in the current batch were done, we said the chunk was GETS. If we had enough GETS software by December 1st then we would ship it. The question was, which one of our factory's machines—the testers, analysts, developers, managers—was the bottleneck? Or was it somewhere or someone else?

Phil arrived before I finished my coffee, effortlessly jogging to the same peak I'd just slogged my way up to. He wore a T-shirt that read "I wish I could change the world, but they won't give me the source code." We politely insulted each other (as men in this part of the world do to demonstrate friendship) while he warmed down. He soon sat, and I brought him up to date on my discussion with Cheryl.

"You want me to sit atop of a hill on a beautiful sunny morning and chat about management theory? Why not! But first things first. Is that coffee down there mine?"

I passed it to him.

"Hmm. It's warm – ish," He took a sip and smiled. "And free. How can I help?"

"Well, first off, do you think the bottleneck concept applies to us?"

"Why wouldn't it?"

I said that—obviously—FPP was a project, not a factory, nor an accounts department, nor a restaurant. They were very different environments with different types of people working in them. Factories and restaurants both have many physical things flowing through them, but the stuff that flows through software projects is "soft," if not invisible: emails and printouts containing knowledge and ideas; code made up of databases and source code; bits and bytes, not atoms.

Phil pulled a light jacket from his backpack and put it on. "None of that matters. It's still about information flow and processes. We must have a bottleneck."

I said, "I reckon we've got five choices: analysts, testers, developers, managers or customers. One of them must have less capacity relative to all the others."

"Agreed, though it could also be our build machines or our test environments. Now zip it old man, and let me think."

And that's what he did. He sat back, closed his eyes, and thought. And then he thought some more. And then, I assume, some more.

Me? I enjoyed the view. I could see the boundaries of the entire city. Mountains in the east, the river and toll bridge in the northwest; the Castle defending its own peak in the southwest corner of the park. Just in front of me, the peak fell away into a cliff. Sports fields, a running track, and tennis courts sat below the cliff. Tourist trams circled the park's perimeter. They were, the tourist pamphlets said, a reminder of days gone by.

Phil cleared his throat. "Okay, I've just run a few thought experiments assuming that, by some miracle, we added more people to each role. I then asked myself if the project ran any faster. And for three of the roles, it didn't."

"Ah ha."

"Analysts aren't our bottleneck. Most of our analysis is already done, and the analysts even have spare capacity to help with testing. It's not our customers either, for much the same reasons. And, I'll tell you for free that we ain't got no shortage of managers."

"Charming," I said. "So, that leaves the developers or the testers."

"Yep. That's where I'm stuck. If we added more testers, we would execute more tests and identify more defects, right? But finding defects sooner doesn't get us to December 1st any quicker unless we can fix them too. I can't decide whether we'd fix the new defects or whether they'd just build up because we didn't have enough developers."

I said, "If we can fix defects faster than we find them, then our testers are the bottleneck, otherwise, it's the developers."

"Ah ha." He held up a single finger to shush me and disappeared into thought for another couple minutes.

"I know where our bottleneck used to be," he said.

"Used to be?"

"In our first chunk, it was definitely our developers. We found dozens of defects, but we could only fix a fraction of them. Developers were definitely our bottleneck then. But things have changed. Now we're fixing defects at about the same rate we can find them. We see that in Tim's daily testing reports."

"So, we have two bottlenecks? Testers and developers."

"Yeah. I think so."

Damn. I knew our situation was more complicated than an accounting department or a cafeteria.

"Would you say the testers are currently finding it harder to find new defects than they did a few weeks ago?" Phil asked.

"According to Tim's testing reports, they are."

"Have you noticed if the newer defects are easier to fix, compared to those we found a few weeks ago?

I shook my head and shrugged. I wasn't close enough to the work to know.

"Trust me, they are. Soon, we'll be able to fix defects faster than we can find them and retest them. I'm sure of that."

"Our testers will soon become our bottleneck?" We were transitioning between the two states, like water turning to ice.

He went quiet for a few seconds. "No, no, no. It's worse than I thought. The testers are about to get a whole lot busier than we ever expected."

I flinched. "You think they're going to unearth more bugs?"

"No. But each day that goes by they'll have to do more regression testing."

"Damn. You're right." Regression testing is when we check we haven't broken anything while changing our software. It was an obvious overhead cost of doing more, smaller batches, and the overhead increased with every new batch. I shook my head, embarrassed. "I should have thought of it."

Phil said, "It doesn't matter. Our regression effort is about to explode. Testing is about to become our bottleneck."

"This sucks."

His eyes widened. "It doesn't suck! This is awesome. If we can squeeze a twenty percent improvement out of testing, then our entire project runs twenty percent faster. Our entire project! That's brilliant news. We now know where to focus, so we're not only going to get faster, but we just got wiser too!"

I nodded, though I didn't share his enthusiasm. "I guess. Rather than figure out how to make everyone more efficient, we only need to figure out how to make our testers more efficient."

"It's more than that, Steve. I need to slow my developers down, so they run at the same speed as the testers. We can't have them running out ahead."

"What? Seriously?"

"Seriously!"

I should my head, incredulous. "You want the developers to just sit around doing nothing?"

He shrugged in a don't-shoot-the-messenger way. "Would you prefer we keep them fixing bugs, even though we don't have the capacity to retest them? All that will do is build up a pile of half-done work. It won't make us go any faster. And we cannot ship untested defects, unless you suddenly want to start producing non-GETS software? Tell me you don't want that."

"I won't do that." I shook my head. "But I also don't want our expensive developers sitting around doing nothing."

"We might have to release some of them back into the developer pool."

"No way."

"Well, we'd best find something else for them to do then."

Neither of us spoke for a minute. Thinking.

I broke the silence with an awkward question. "Are you willing to let your developers do testing?"

"They already do a lot of testing, lots and lots of testing."

"I don't mean normal developer testing. I mean would you let them work as part of the test team, following the test team's rules?"

He blanched. "No."

"You'd rather they sit on their hands and do nothing?"

He shook his head. "I'd rather we use their developer brains rather than their fingertips."

"Doing what?"

"I'm not sure. Maybe they can automate some things that make the testers more productive." He shrugged. "I'll need to talk to my guys, and to Tim and his guys too."

As we walked back to the office, we agreed the obvious thing to do was to eliminate, or reduce, anything that wasted tester time. Cancelling all non-essential meetings was a no-brainer, but Phil also thought we could reduce testers' waiting time by doing code builds more frequently. The build schedule was set up to minimize his developers' downtime, but his team could change things so the testers' downtime was minimized instead, even if it meant his developers were less productive.

When we hit High Street, I asked him if he knew about how Krzysztof, Sharon and Brian talked about their test scenarios before executing their tests. I'd been so busy with Gregor that I hadn't had a chance to share what they did. I explained, and he agreed that we should get the other teams working that way.

I told him how Eleanor had berated me in front of Craig and my junior staff.

"Ouch."

"It does make me wonder if the other teams have also come up with good ideas they haven't shared yet. We've changed their way of working significantly, and they're bound to have adapted their working practices."

"I'll ask around."

When we reached the office, Phil went to talk to Tim and I

went to talk to Catherine and Gregor. We agreed to meet up again later today, before lunch.

CHAPTER FORTY-TWO

I found Catherine sitting in my office chair, a water bottle beside her, her laptop open.

She did not look happy.

She rose out of my chair when she saw me, waving a scrunched-up sheet of paper. "Chaste issued a press release at close of business last night."

I reclaimed my chair. "Good morning."

"I am not happy."

She dumped her anger on me. Chaste was now launching on December 1st. Their product was similar to ours, but considerably smaller, despite our descoping exercises. As far as she could tell, they didn't have Catherine's most desired feature: customer-level income. But nor did we, so that one was a draw. Their proposition was mostly self-service, relying on customers looking after themselves through a web app. Our proposition was full service, and although FPP would have some pretty web pages, we didn't have a web app. We would, of course, play our full service as a benefit, but no web app made us look weak.

"So actually, although I'm angry at Chaste, there are no surprises and at least we know where we stand. We have similar offerings, but we appeal to different markets. It's not all bad news."

"That's good," I said, "because I have some. Bad news, I mean."

She sat. She knew what was coming.

"We're not even going to make December 1st, are we?"

I shook my head and briefly described my weekend of spreadsheet hell with Gregor.

She looked at the ceiling as she absorbed what I'd just told her. "But there is a slim chance?"

"Yes, but too slim to count on."

She nodded. "What are the chances we'll ship something that will stand on its own before March?"

"Middling to good."

She said, "Mark told me December 1st has to be a slam dunk, or otherwise there will be consequences. He said we have to be selling FPP to real customers on December 1st for it to count."

"As it stands, we cannot do that."

She looked like she was in pain. "You need to tell Eleanor and I need to tell Mark so they can break the news to Hal."

I leaned forward and asked quietly, "Can you hold off a few hours?"

She looked at me suspiciously. "Why?"

"We have an idea that might make things better." I explained how testers were about to become our bottleneck and how maybe we could come up with something to speed them up.

"Testers?"

"A ten percent increase in testing capacity makes the whole project run ten percent faster."

Her eyes widened. "I'm sure Mark can find budget to recruit more testers." She reached for her mobile.

I shook my head and explained how adding new people to the project at this late stage would almost certainly slow the project down. I added that I was getting together with Phil and Tim later to figure out what the whole team could do to squeeze more out of our testing.

"Is it worth it?" she said. "Can we realistically speed things up enough to hit December 1st?"

I said, "I doubt it," which was true. "But we won't know until we try. We'd have to at least double, or triple, our current speed before December 1st is guaranteed. I can't see that happening."

She said, "Look, don't be offended by me asking this, but can I look at the spreadsheet you and Gregor used to come up with your dates? I trust your work, but you never know. With fresh eyes I might see something you've missed."

I was about to say that we'd double-checked our work, but who was I to stop her clutching at straws?

I made a copy of the spreadsheet which she opened on her laptop, and then I quickly walked her through the structure. I asked her to not play around with the macros. Gregor and I knew how to work them, but they hadn't been built for sharing. I suggested she work in my office since Gregor sat just around the corner, and he could dig her out of any quicksand if she got bogged down in the spreadsheet. Besides, I had some other things I needed to do. It was 8:20 a.m.

CHAPTER FORTY-THREE

The stuff I needed to do was go away and think by myself. And get more coffee.

I stopped by Gregor's desk on the way to the canteen and quickly explained that Catherine was looking at his spreadsheet and how testing was our bottleneck.

He nodded. "It's like in that book, *The Goal.*"

I looked at him, surprised. "You've read the book?"

"My MBA contained a short module on the Theory of Constraints."

"Theory of Constraints?"

"It's the theory underlying the ideas in *The Goal.* The gist is that you make a chain stronger by making its weakest link stronger. Strengthening any other link makes the chain heavier, but not stronger."

I crouched down beside him and asked, quietly, "If you knew we needed to go faster, Gregor, why didn't you mention the book?"

He looked confused by my question at first, then indignant. "Honestly, Steve? That was a long time ago. Interesting book, I suppose, but it's about manufacturing and I've never worked in a factory. Do you really think we can use the ideas here?"

"Definitely," I said, surprised at my own confidence. "We're pretty sure that testing is about to become our bottleneck. Phil and Tim are meeting at 11:00 to figure out how the developers and testers can help."

"Do you want me to meet them?"

I thought a moment. "No, not yet. I'd prefer you stay here and help Catherine out with your spreadsheet, if she needs it. I've no idea if she will come up with anything, but who knows?"

"Okay. But let me know if you need me."

"Of course."

I thanked him, then headed downstairs to the canteen where I mulled over another cup of coffee, thought about rowboats, and came up with a good idea.

CHAPTER FORTY-FOUR

I settled on tea, figuring I'd already had too much coffee. I drank it in the darkest corner of the staff cafeteria, carefully avoiding eye contact, just wanting quiet time either to think or to not think, I wasn't sure which. After half an hour of thinking and not thinking, I headed back to my office. I was still a good ten feet away when I heard Gregor exclaim, "Are you nuts?"

My door was closed.

I gingerly tapped on it, then nudged it open. "Who's nuts?"

No one answered, so I ventured in. Gregor was leaning against the wall, his neck red. Catherine sat with her laptop open in front of her, looking defiant.

"Gregor thinks I am crazy." She shrugged. "But, if he were to hear me out, he would discover that I am freakily sane."

Gregor let out a long breath through pursed lips.

She pointed at her laptop screen. "Do you want to see why?"

I pulled my desk chair over to the table and sat down.

"Gregor filtered my copy of your spreadsheet to highlight work with the highest test effort."

I frowned. "You wanted to see what features use most of our bottleneck resource?"

"I want to slash any test-heavy scope, if I can, and save us that testing effort."

Now I knew why Gregor was angry. "How can you possibly do that when you've already cut the scope to its barest bones?"

"Things change." She shrugged. "I can't speed your team up, but maybe I can shorten our journey."

Gregor grunted. "True, but you're going too far." Maybe I didn't understand why he was angry after all.

She ignored him and pointed at the screen. "These are all of the test scenarios needed for the Search screen. It's a busy screen, with many combinations, and it requires a lot of testing. I'm comfortable going live with just a subset and then adding others later, if we need them, after December. Understand?"

"Ah ha."

She said, "Initially, I figured we only needed surname, date of birth, account number, and post code for launch, but then I got brutally honest with myself and decided I only need one search field. That's when Gregor went nuts."

"Just one field?" I glanced at Gregor, who raised his eyebrows. "Which field?"

Catherine folded her arms. "Surname."

"You're nuts!"

I heard Gregor mumble, "That's what I said."

"I'm not. I'm talking about what we need for when we go live. Let me ask you, Steve, realistically, how many people are going to buy our product in December and January and February?"

I said, "A few thousand?"

"Let's say we strike gold and it's five thousand. Every customer knows their own surname, and worst case we might have a few dozen Smiths and Jones and McDonalds. My staff can search by surname then scroll and scan, as need be."

I said, "Okay…"

"Then, in January, I'll ask my staff what fields they desperately need next and I'll ask you to add them."

Gregor now looked as if he wished he'd let Catherine explain her rationale before reacting. He mumbled, "It doesn't sound so bad when you put it that way."

I nodded. "We'll add them in phase two and you can get them in, say, March." I mulled on that a moment. In my head I still had it that December through March we'd be nursing FPP into life, like we usually did. But if we could both run faster and shorten the journey while still building GETS software, then that wasn't the case anymore.

Catherine said, "After we've launched, we'll ask which gaps most need plugging. We'll plug them, and keep doing that until we run out of budget." She turned to me. "That's how it will work, right?"

I said, "Yeah, of course," though truthfully I'd not thought that far ahead. "We'll use phase two to enhance the product and to fix any urgent defects."

"Good. In that case, Gregor, can you defer these search scenarios?"

Gregor updated the spreadsheet and ran a macro that recalculated the plan. Our earliest possible date had shimmied back almost a week.

"We hit pay dirt, boys," Catherine said. "Shall I keep digging?"

CHAPTER FORTY-FIVE

I arrived at the conference room at exactly 11 a.m. Phil and Tim were already there. Phil had tied a knot in Fippy the Snake's tail and was making *yee-ha* noises as he twirled him over his head like a lasso.

We sat and I told them about Catherine's descoping of the search features.

Phil said, "What stopped her doing that months ago?"

I said, "Maybe she wasn't desperate enough? Plus, last time we descoped we asked her to prioritize features. But this time, with the search feature, she's trimmed a five-star solution for an existing feature down to a one-star solution."

Phil said, "Whatever the reason, that's awesome news let's hope she keeps slashing. But now, on to more important and—dare I say it?—more interesting things!" He rested Fippy on the table. "We haven't had a lot of time, but Tim and I have come up with a few ways to increase our testing capacity quickly, none of which involve chucking more testers at the problem or lowering quality. Some of our ideas are obvious, some of them are ... not quite so obvious."

Tim said, "Let's start with the four most obvious ideas. First, we'll cut unnecessary and over-long meetings. Second, we'll rollout Kryz, Sharon and Brian's pre-test discussion to all the other teams. Third—"

I said, "You heard about that?"

"Yeah," he said, then averted his gaze for a moment. "Sharon updated me on Friday afternoon. Third, we will start doing a little look ahead and batching up some tests. Fourth, we will—"

"Hang on," I said. "You want to increase the batch size? Isn't that the exact opposite of what we want to do?"

Tim shook his head. "I shouldn't think so. Not if it makes our bottleneck team faster. It's often quicker to execute tests A, B and C together as one batch, rather than do each in isolation. Why? Because the output of A is the input to B, and so on. Make sense?"

I checked with Phil, who nodded. "We're not talking about doing bigger batches, just selecting what we work on now so it makes more efficient use of the tester's time."

"Okay."

"And fourth, we will stop our developers from batching up their fixes. Rather than dumping a batch of, say, twenty fixes every third day, we want them to drip feed the fixes, for retesting, several times a day."

"Phil mentioned this possibility," I said.

Tim said, "Developers are non-bottlenecks, so by definition they have spare capacity. We should use that spare capacity to do more releases. More releases will improve the flow of work to the testing team and it'll keep the testers busy. As it is, they are often blocked while they wait for fixes to be released."

"Also," Phil said, "if we drip feed the defects rather than releasing twenty fixes in one burst, then the test guys can get cleverer and more focused about their regression testing."

I said, "Makes sense, but I have one concern. More releases will require more coordination between the teams, right?"

"Yes, we will have more releases so we'll have to coordinate those more carefully. But, equally, each release will be much smaller so they should be easier to coordinate."

"Okay."

Phil waited a moment to see if I had any more questions, then said, "Now for the less obvious suggestions. Prepare yourself to be shocked."

I made a show of pretending to brace myself.

Tim sat upright in his chair before he spoke. "This *will* shock you, Steve. I promise you. But it seems like a good idea."

I smiled politely, humoring him. "I'm ready."

"It pains me, but we should temporarily disband FPP's automated testing team."

I raised my eyebrows, shook my head, and dropped my jaw—all at the same time. It's possible some drool dripped out the side of my mouth. He was kidding me, right? That team automated much of the testing that would otherwise be done manually. They created a bunch of incredibly cheap, reliable, digital robots who tapped away at FPP's software making sure it worked as defined, much like our manual testers did, but they did it in the middle of the night and without bio breaks or complaining. Tim had fought hard to form and protect the team. But now, here he was, offering to close it down.

"Surely we need more automated testing now, not less?"

"Yes, but right now, we're doing the wrong sort of automated testing. We're still creating FPP, so its user interface keeps changing, sometimes a dozen times a day, and since our automated tests work through the user interface, they keep breaking. Accordingly, I've got my four most skilled and knowledgeable testers working full-time fixing broken test scripts. I'd rather we abandon the tests temporarily, since they're basically useless, then fix them later, when the UI stabilizes."

I nodded slowly, considering what he'd just said. "We'd increase our manual test capacity from twenty to twenty-four, which is at least a twenty percent increase." Nice.

"No, Phil and I think we can use those guys more cleverly than that," Tim said.

Phil said, "We've got a better idea. Actually, there's a word for it ..." But then he stopped talking because he couldn't think of the word. "It's the phenomenon of when you add one plus one and get three."

"Synergy?"

"That's it. We want to pair each freed-up tester with a developer and use the synergy of their combined tester and developer brain power. Developers know and can do and see stuff that testers can't. Testers know and can do and see stuff that developers can't. We've not had a lot of time to think about this, but we've already thought of three ways we can get synergy by getting testers and developers working together."

"Tell me more."

Tim said, "Here's the first one. My testers understand the data and the application better than the developers, but Phil's developers understand the code. We want to pair two of them up and automate the creation of some of our most useful test data."

I nodded.

"Our data-setup team's work is manual and a little error-prone. If we automate some of their work then we could use some of the folk on that team to do manual testing."

Phil said, "We'll start with the low-hanging fruit—the most common tasks that take the most time when done manually—and can have the first of them automated within a couple of days."

"That's ... ambitious. Are you sure?"

Phil's face reddened a little. "Yeah ... well, see, a good bit of the code is already built. Me and my developers, we're lazy, so we automate time-consuming and repetitive stuff, like data setup, whenever we can. It's just what we do. We just never thought to share our hand-cranked tools with Tim's team."

"To be fair, we never asked," Tim said. "That should free up maybe three to five data-setup staff to execute manual regression tests."

"How much extra test capacity will that give us?"

Tim screwed up his face. "Maybe ten or twenty percent? The people we free up aren't our strongest testers, but they can do some of the easier stuff, which will free up the more skilled guys to do the harder stuff."

I nodded with what I hoped looked like a serious look on my face. Secretly though, on the inside I was dancing. Ten percent extra bottleneck capacity made the entire project run ten percent faster. "Okay. You said there were three examples of synergy. What's next?"

"This one is something we probably should have done from the start of the project," Phil said. "We want to pair up another tester and developer and automate the testing of FPP's calculation engine."

Tim said, "It takes up a lot of my team's time, is painfully error-prone and none of them like it."

I nodded. The calculation engine was the most important bit of the entire solution to get right.

Phil said, "But since it's an algorithm, with inputs and expected outputs, it's straight-forward to automate. If Tim's team prepares a spreadsheet table of inputs and expected results, we'll create a test harness which hooks directly into the calculation engine. We will run several days' worth of manual testing in several minutes, several times a day if we want."

I saw a red flag. "Why will this work, when the UI-based automation doesn't?"

Phil smiled. "The calcs are stable, the user interface isn't. Plus, we'll hook the testing harness directly into the depths of the code, totally avoiding the UI. The UI can keep changing, but it won't affect our tests."

"Okay," I said. "And let me guess. You already have a test harness in place which you can share with the testers for free?"

"Nope. But we can build one quickly."

"Good. And the third?"

"You know how, until recently, our two teams have worked separately?" Tim said. "Well, working separately resulted in some duplicated testing. We think we can eliminate some of that now that we are working together."

"What? Why on earth would we do duplicate testing at all?"

"When a developer fixes a defect, they do their own testing and then hand it over to my testers who do *their* own testing. They assume the developer has done a good job, but they start with a blank slate. So, sometimes the testers repeat some testing the developers have already done. When they worked separately that made sense, but now we can remove some of the overlap."

"Okay," I said. "Are you sure you can do this without cutting corners?"

Tim's eyes narrowed and I realized I'd inadvertently questioned his and his team's professionalism. They'd never suggest anything they thought jeopardized quality. I tried to recover from my misstep. "So ... do you think we could, maybe, trial this with Kryz, Sharon and Brian's team before rolling it out to the other teams?"

Tim said, "Of course."

I nodded. "How much extra testing capacity will this create?"

Tim said, "My gut says between ten and thirty percent, so, say twenty percent?"

I said, "I'll assume ten. Anything else?"

Tim said, "Not yet. But this is surely enough to get us started."

I thought a moment. "It's a good start." Which it was, but I knew it wasn't enough.

I knew I needed to be pessimistic about the potential, but I figured their changes would give us at least fifty percent improvement in test-team throughput, which meant the whole team would run fifty percent faster. Though we could well get considerably more.

That leap in performance seemed both outrageous and conservative at the same time. Outrageous because, normally, we viewed a fifteen percent improvement as impressive; conservative because I'd consciously rounded down. We still had two ex-UI automation testers up our sleeves and the three of us had only spent a few hours thinking about this. I knew our teams would come up with more innovations, over time, though we couldn't afford to overwhelm ourselves with too many changes at once.

I frowned, "You know, all of these suggestions seem really smart and achievable, but if they're so smart, how come we've never done them before?"

Tim shrugged. "We never knew we had a bottleneck before, so previously we tried to keep both our teams running as fast as they could. That, I guess, was suboptimal, because sometimes improvements in one team deteriorated performance in another."

Phil said, "Now that we know we have a bottleneck, we know we have to manage things differently; to look at the whole, not just the parts."

"Okay," I said. "Now I have a suggestion. What do you call the person who sits at the back of the boat in those rowing boat races, the ones between Cambridge and Oxford University?"

Phil said, "The one they throw in the water at the end of a regatta?"

"Yeah."

"It's the coxswain. I think."

"That's the one," I said. "We need to get ourselves some coxswains."

Neither spoke.

"The coxswain adds weight and doesn't row. Right? So why have them?"

Phil said, "They steer, don't they?"

I nodded.

"And they keep the individual rowers rowing in sync," Tim added.

I said, "And they also provide a bit of motivation by keeping the pressure on."

Phil looked doubtful. "And you think we to need get ourselves some coxswains? To do the coordination work?"

I nodded.

"Don't Tim, Anne and I already do that?"

I said, "Sort of. You manage the staff in your specialties, and that worked fine before. But now that the teams are multi-functional and collaborate much more, we need someone in each team who coordinates the work of the team."

Tim said, "Like mini-project managers?"

I nodded. "Like that, but focusing on the internal working of the team, rather than the external stuff. Gregor does all the external stuff, but doesn't have enough time to coordinate all the work inside the teams." I thought a moment, then added, "And if he did, it'd look like he was micro-managing."

Tim said, "Some of the teams are struggling. There's a lot more coordination required than they're used to."

Phil said, "Yeah, but others are doing okay."

"Why is that?"

He shrugged. "I guess some teams just got lucky and ended up with a self-appointed coordinator inside the team. Some people are just naturally good at that sort of stuff and they can't help themselves."

I said, "So maybe we need to recognize those people for what they're already doing and then figure out how to help the other teams do the same? They might have someone in the team who just needs permission to take on the coxswain work. Or we might need to provide someone."

Phil said, "I buy all that, except for one thing. We need to find a better name than coxswain."

We spent a minute discussing possible names for the role. I decided to steal Craig Lally's job title and call them flowmasters.

With that settled, Tim and Phil agreed they'd get together with Gregor and Anne to choose the new flowmasters and to figure out what the job entailed and offer coaching.

I excused myself, leaving the other two to start rolling out our changes, and returned to my office, hoping that Catherine had managed to thin the product out even further.

CHAPTER FORTY-SIX

I returned to my office and found Vrinda sitting next to Catherine. They appeared deep in conversation around my laptop. I fake-coughed and they looked up.

Vrinda smiled. "At last! Our white knight has returned! Pull up a pew. We have a disaster."

I pulled my chair over. "Disaster?"

"We have brutally sliced and diced the spreadsheet until the bare bones product not only has no meat on it, it's missing a few important bones."

"Ouch ..." I wasn't sure if she thought that was a good thing or a bad thing.

"Don't worry, it's still good enough to go live—barely. Provided we keep adding bones, then muscle and so forth after. Problem is, we can't prune much more and we don't know if it's enough. We're not brave enough to run your macro."

Catherine said, "You said not to. And Gregor is in a meeting."

Now that was the sort of disaster I knew I could handle. I said I would show them, but I asked to hear more about their updates, first. There was no rush, I said.

That wasn't true. I desperately wanted to reach across the table and grab the laptop, bumping up our execution speed by fifty percent. But I held back lest I blunt Catherine's enthusiasm for slicing and dicing.

"I'll start with the bad news," Catherine said, "which is that we got lucky when I picked the Search feature and none of the other features can be thinned out nearly as much. The good news is, we did discard roughly a fifth of the scenarios across the other features."

"That *is* good."

"There's more, but first let me ask you something."

"Okay."

"How would you feel, Steve, if we launched without the statement feature in place, but delivered it by early January? Our first statement run is mid-January."

I checked Catherine's laptop to see how much work was involved. Roughly one to two weeks, assuming it wasn't full of bugs. "It's doable, but with the holiday break at the end of December, it'd need to be the first thing we started working on after launch."

Vrinda said, "The thirty-day penalty-free cancelation period is similar, and there are a few other Day Two scenarios like that."

Catherine nodded. "We have four Day Two scenarios and a bunch of others which must be live before sales warm up in March. And we've clearly identified a lot of features and scenarios that must be live on December 1st, as well as a whole other bunch which we might need, but we might not."

"Got an example?"

"A lot of them are processes which we'd prefer were all automated, but we might survive if some weren't."

"Like?"

She waved her hand in front of me, as if it were obvious. "We could use the existing cumbersome refunds process, if we don't have to do many refunds. But if we do get a lot of refunds, then we'd need to automate the process or recruit more CSRs just to do that process. Trouble is, right now we've got no way of knowing how many refunds we'll get."

"Okay."

Catherine said, "I'm calling this bunch 'demand-based,' and I'm guessing we'll need a third of them. Though since I don't know which third, I'm very happy to launch without them, provided you set aside a fixed percentage of your team's capacity to build them based on demand."

I bit down on my lip, then smiled to myself. "You mean, you want to wing it?"

Catherine furrowed her brow. "That's not how I'd describe it, but yes, I suppose so. We'll 'wing it,' but in a disciplined and planned way. Assuming Eleanor approves more budget in April, then I'd like to run that way until the money runs out."

I said good, and it *was* good. Not just for FPP, but for me, too. For the first time in my career, one of my customers had requested we work to a fixed budget, variable scope promise. Who'd have thought?

Also, from what I'd heard I suspected Catherine and Vrinda had prioritized FPP's scope enough that, combined with our bottleneck improvements, we might just make it.

Feeling rather pleased, I decided it was time to put them—and me—out of our misery.

I reached across the table to the laptop and kicked off the recalculation macro that Gregor had built. I clicked the summary tab, frowned when I saw the results.

The earliest date we could ship the bare bones scenarios occurred in the second week of November, but the most likely delivery date was mid-December.

I hadn't adjusted our speed yet, however.

We'd made it.

But I didn't smile, even though that was the exact moment I stopped worrying about FPP. I chose not to put Catherine and Vrinda out of their misery because I knew that if I did, Catherine would stop her slicing and dicing. I didn't know what clever ideas hadn't been found yet for lack of hunting, but I knew that they were there. I didn't want to remove the pressure, the desperation.

I turned the laptop screen to face them and waited for their reaction.

"Wow." Vrinda shook her head in amazement. "We've now got good odds of delivering by December 1st. That's brilliant!"

Catherine's reaction was different. She dropped her head down until her chin rested on her chest. She closed her eyes. Her hair fell down over her face and I heard her mumbled words. "This isn't good enough. December 1st needs to be a definite—a slam dunk."

Vrinda broke the silence about a minute later. "There must be more we can do."

Catherine lifted her head and brushed her hair away. "Perhaps, but I don't know where else to look."

None of us spoke.

Catherine said, "I need to make a call." She grabbed her phone from her handbag and left the office.

Vrinda and I poked around inside the spreadsheet while she was gone, but didn't come up with any new ideas.

"Right!" Catherine said as she rejoined us at the table. "Are either of you familiar with the concept of customer segmentation?"

We both nodded. Vrinda said, "It's where marketing divides their customers up into different groups, like DINKIES—Double Income No Kids, and YUPPIES—Young Urban Professionals. Each segment has different needs, so clever businesses treat them differently."

Catherine nodded. "Mark suggests we segment the product to allow us to launch FPP to fewer customer segments, provided we add others later. With me?"

We both nodded.

Catherine said, "One brute-force and unimaginative segmentation might be new customers; another would be existing customers."

Vrinda said, "We could save a lot of pre-December work if we only take on existing Wyx-group customers. Credit checking, for instance. We haven't even started testing that yet."

"Alternatively, we could delay our migration work if we only took on new customers," Catherine said.

"Other segments are people who aren't retiring in the next five years, people who are retiring soon, and people who've already retired. Each segment has quite different processes."

I smiled and said, "You know, if we didn't sell the product in Wales, we could avoid the Welsh language customizations. It's a small thing from a development perspective, but it'd simplify testing."

"You want to start a civil war with the Welsh?" said Catherine, before rattling off another three ways we could potentially slice and dice our customers. So to speak.

We spent a few minutes debating our options before Catherine said she simply had to call Mark in since these types of decisions were way above her pay grade.

I waved away the suggestion. "Let's do that tomorrow."

Catherine's head jerked up. "No. Today. We've not got time to waste."

I shook my head. "No." I tried to suppress my smile, but failed. "We've no need to rush."

Her eyes narrowed. "Why?"

"Watch." I turned her laptop to face me, but when I tapped the key it asked for Catherine's password, which dulled the spectacle somewhat. But within thirty seconds, I'd clicked the spreadsheet tab holding Gregor's and my assumptions and bumped our assumed speed up by half for each of the best, most likely, and worst case scenarios.

As Catherine watched, she said, "You arse. You lied to us."

I switched back to the summary tab and hovered the mouse over the macro button. I looked at them both. "Are you guys ready?"

They nodded. All three of us leaned in closer to the screen.

I clicked the macro, and with just the merest pause, the numbers changed. We had our slam dunk.

Catherine's jaw fell open and she leaned in closer to the screen, blinking as if she could not believe her eyes. "No way! No way! No way!"

Vrinda looked at the screen, then to me, then back to the screen, then back to me. "We've made it? We've really made it?"

I nodded. "We've made it."

CHAPTER FORTY-SEVEN

An hour later I stood, for the second time that day, atop Kelvin's peak. I was puffing from the climb. I'd taken the slow, hard route to get there, climbing the paths worn over the years into the cliff face rather than the asphalt path. My brain was buzzing.

We would deliver FPP on December 1st! It would be bare, bare bones, in need of a good feed and a long relaxing bath and a pep talk to boost its self-esteem, but it would be healthy, not riddled with bugs, and we would start filling in the biggest gaps as soon as we launched. Most importantly, Hal and Eleanor would keep their promise, and we'd avoided the unpleasant, though unnamed, consequences of failing to keep that promise.

I'd called Phil, Gregor and Tim into my office where I let Catherine and Vrinda enjoy the pleasure of sharing our good news. Being sensible folk, we'd agreed to take a few hours out, let things consolidate in our minds, then regroup at 4 p.m. with clearer heads. Provided we still felt good after that meeting, I'd speak to Eleanor and Catherine would speak to Mark.

It was the sensible thing to do, really. Really, it was.

Catherine had gone off to her office. Vrinda had gone off to speak with Phil, Tim and Gregor. And I took a long hard climb up a steep hill.

I looked around me. The bench where Phil and I sat earlier that morning was occupied by a Mom and her two kids, one just a baby sitting in a stroller, the other a toddler sitting on the bench beside his mom, swinging his little legs in front of him. I sat on a seat-shaped rock near the cliff edge. School kids wearing brightly colored sports uniforms played hockey in the fields below.

I'd bought a cheese baguette on the way there. I bit off a chunk and washed it down with some water.

I turned my face towards the sun, closed my eyes and thought of precisely nothing.

I heard shouts from the hockey game below me, and the occasional seagull squawked from above.

I let the pleasant calmness linger for as long as I could until I broke my promise to Catherine and Vrinda. I pulled out my phone and dialed Eleanor.

As I waited for her to answer, I picked a pebble from the ground beside my rock and gently flicked it over the edge of the cliff face. I leaned forward and watched it effortlessly bounce its way down, down, down into the brush at the bottom.

Interesting. Gravity didn't always suck.

CHAPTER FORTY-EIGHT

"Eleanor Scharlau speaking. How may I help you?"

"It's Steve. I have some good news for you, Eleanor."

"I heard. From Mark. And I have some questions for you."

So much for the "well dones" and "thank yous." And so much for Catherine's vow of silence.

"Okay."

"I need to calibrate your confidence level. Answer honestly. Will you take a one hundred pound bet against me that you will go live on December 1st and Mark will get everything you've promised?"

Strange question, but I answered without thinking. "Of course."

One hundred pounds was a nice dinner for two. Not that I had anyone to eat it with.

"One thousand pounds?"

I paused before answering. That was a reasonable amount of money, a very nice new television. "Of course."

"Ten thousand pounds?"

I bit down on my lip. Serious money. If Fran were still alive, she would get very grumpy if ten grand suddenly disappeared from our check account. That was enough to buy a small but zippy new car.

"Is this for real? Or are you asking me hypothetically?"

"Answer the bloody question."

"I'd take that bet, and before you ask," —I felt myself getting annoyed—"I would happily bet one million pounds, but only hypothetically. I'd feel awkward taking your money."

"That's what I wanted to hear. Good work." Then a pause. "Honestly, Steven? I didn't think you had it in you."

"Gee thanks, Eleanor."

"Tell me the details."

So I did. I talked. She listened.

I was still talking ten minutes later when Eleanor cut in—it was the first time she had said anything besides the occasional *um-hum* and *I see*. "Hold the line please, Steven."

Abruptly, I found myself listening to Wyx-Fin's hold music.

Three minutes later I was still on hold, so I muted my mobile phone, put it on speaker and rested it on the rock beside me.

I checked that the phone was definitely on mute, then said out loud, "Steve, you are awesome." Just because I was alone and I could. I figured I'd earned that pleasure.

I took a few nibbles from my baguette as I waited.

I heard a man shouting behind me. I turned and saw a black Labrador bounding towards me, chasing a tennis ball. Behind him, an elderly gentleman carrying the dog's lead hobbled towards us. The dog raced past me, caught the ball mid-bounce and turned and raced back towards the man. They played tug of war with the ball for a few moments before the man pulled the ball away and tossed it in the opposite direction. The dog took off after the ball with the old man following along behind, barely able to keep up.

As I waited, I thought about how our news changed things. A few hours earlier, FPP was a failing project, and I was failing with it. But now FPP was succeeding and I was looking—and feeling—somewhat heroic. Heroic and exhausted. I needed a holiday. I owed my kids a holiday. We all needed a rest.

Finally the music stopped and Eleanor came back on the line.

"Steven. Hal and Mark are here. I'm putting you on speaker."

I quickly picked up the phone and switched off mute and the speaker. "Hal, Mark."

"Abernethy," said Hal, gruffly.

"Steve," said Mark.

Hal said, "Is it true what Mark and Eleanor tell me? We will ship on December 1st?"

"Yes."

"Do you have any doubts at all? Think carefully before you answer."

"None."

"Okay. Tell me this then. In return for this certainty, are you delivering me a half-arsed product?"

"Mark and Catherine should judge that, not me."

"They tell me FPP is considerably smaller than intended, but in some ways better, simpler. Makes me suspicious. Sounds like they're blowing smoke up my kilt. I want to know two things. Is it worthy of the great Wyx-Fin brand and will customers buy it. Mark tells me the answers are yes and yes. But he would, wouldn't he? What do *you* think, Abernethy?"

I didn't imagine he valued my opinion, but I answered directly nonetheless. "I'd buy the product. And I'd recommend my friends buy it too."

He said nothing for a moment. "Then, in that case, so will I." His voice got quieter, as if he had turned away from the speaker phone. "There you go Mark. I've just made your first two sales for you."

I heard Mark say thanks, though I don't think he meant it.

Just before the hold music came on again, I heard Hal say faintly, "Maybe there is hope ..."

A few minutes later Eleanor took me off hold. "We're alone again."

"Hal seems happy."

"Shush now, though. Give me a minute to think."

CHAPTER FORTY-NINE

A seagull squawked above me.

I tore a crust off my baguette and threw it high in the air towards the bird. It caught it in midair then swooped away without even saying thank you. I named it Hal the Seagull then sat back and waited for it to fly over and poop on my head.

I waited a full minute before Eleanor spoke. "This may change everything. I need to tell you something, Steve. You cannot share it with anyone. Promise me?"

I adjusted myself so I was comfortable on my rock. "I promise."

"I did not believe you would deliver FPP on time. Nor did Hal. Nor anyone in Group. So your good news, while it is good, has taken us by surprise. Do you understand?"

"I understand." I didn't tell her I was probably more surprised than they were.

"FPP was Hal's get-out-of-jail-free card. With that card in question, we were forced to take some drastic actions. FPP may yet save us from having to follow through on them."

She paused.

"Of course, it might not. It all depends on how well FPP sells when we launch. This is very important, Steven, so listen carefully. Do you understand the financial implications of delivering FPP in December?"

I thought a moment before answering. I hadn't expected a quiz.

FPP was a little over its budget, but we always expected that, so I didn't think that was what she was fishing for. On the other hand, previously we'd expected FPP to launch during the summer of next year, if we got lucky, so if we wrapped up FPP in December, that'd save us around eight months.

I said, "FPP development costs a quarter of a million each month. If we finish FPP in December rather than, say, July, we've reduced FPP's development cost by roughly two million pounds. Is that what you're looking for?"

"No. First, there's no way now that we will stop development work on FPP in December. We may shrink the team, but I doubt it. FPP is inadequate and we will continue investing in it, growing it into the type of product we need. Second, while you are correct that if we did stop FPP in December then FPP's costs would be lower, but apart from losing a few contractors your department's overall cost won't drop, because we will start other projects.

"No, Steven, the only thing that matters going forward is how well FPP sells. Now try again. What are the financial implications of delivering early?"

I paused, not knowing where to start.

I heard her sigh. "Let's take this slowly. When Mark first proposed this project, he presented several financial scenarios for the Future Perfect product, each with different assumptions and different cash flow figures. When I say cash flow I mean net cash, the difference between the cash we spend operating the new Future Perfect business and the revenue we receive from our new customers. Understand?"

"Yes."

"Scenario one optimistically assumes Future Perfect will pull in four million pounds a month in net cash after we launch in December. That figure is not what we'd earn from day one, obviously, but it's the average projected over the following three years. The equivalent figure for scenario two was two million. And for scenario three it was only one million. Follow?"

Once again I said yes.

"So, where are we now? Our severely cut-down product looks disturbingly like our aggressive and much loved competitor's, so there's no discernible reason for new customers to prefer ours to theirs. But it's an adequate product and we have a loyal customer base and an effective retail network. So, I pragmatically and pessimistically assume it will pull in a mere half million a month, on average, starting in December. With me?"

"Yes."

"Now, given that's money coming in we didn't have, tell me, what are the financial implications of delivering early?"

My mouth slowly fell open as I crunched the numbers. The math was easy. Eight months unexpected selling, at half a million pounds each month, was four million pounds. That was four million cash in our coffers that wouldn't have been there otherwise.

I, with some help, had just made a significant contribution to the Group's finances.

Wyx-Fin had given a measly three million pounds profit back to Group the previous year, and barely broke even the year before. I knew cash flow numbers didn't translate directly into profit and loss numbers, but delivering FPP early had huge financial implications.

I smiled to myself, but then it occurred to me that Eleanor was treating me like I was some kind of idiot when really I was a hero. I put my tongue firmly into my cheek. "Wow. Two and half million pounds?"

She was silent for a few seconds. "Are you serious?"

"No, of course not. And who'd have thought that a drunken confession from a former employee would cause us to bring us something like four million cash into the company?"

"Who'd have thought, indeed. Halifax thinks it was his inspirational leadership."

"Hal is happy with me then, right?" He should have been. Adding four million extra to his piggy bank was like giving his tarnished career a good spit and polish.

She chuckled. "Hal happy? What an interesting idea. No, he isn't happy. Those drastic actions I can't tell you about are still in play. Is he happy with you? As far as he is concerned, you promised to deliver FPP on February 1st, and pulling the date forward two months was just good management on his part. You're playing with the big boys and girls now, Steve. Get over it."

And then she hung up on me.

The seagull had pooped on me, after all.

Monday, October 16th
FPP launch date - December 1st, this year

CHAPTER FIFTY

I worked with Gregor and the rest of his team for the remainder of that week, and then felt so good about things I took the kids (and my laptop and a backlog of ebooks) to the Canary Islands for a couple of weeks' sunshine. I asked Mom to come along, but she gracefully declined. She didn't say it, but sometimes she needed a break, too.

While I was away I read *The Goal* and re-read *Made to Stick*. I started contemplating how I might rollout some of the lessons we'd learned from FPP to new projects.

When I returned to work the following Monday, just over ten weeks had passed since Phil discovered Chaste's plan, eight weeks since we had inverted FPP, and three weeks since we'd discovered we would—unless something disastrous happened—make our December 1st date.

During those three weeks, Mark and Catherine decided to only sell FPP to existing Wyxcomb customers, which cut our pre-December development effort considerably, and to rollout FPP only to our Scottish Branches before December 1st. We would then rollout to the rest of the country in the new year, which created a little extra work for our development team but gave Catherine's team time to set up her call centers and implement training in the branch in a careful and controlled manner. That said, she was up against the wall and was now the project's critical path. She and her team had a hectic six weeks ahead of them. And after we launched, their workload would be higher than originally expected because she was going live with more manual tasks than planned.

Our initial bottleneck improvement tweaks were bedding in nicely and our newly named flowmasters had created their own simple three-list systems on whiteboards, one per team, which made each team's work visible and easier to coordinate. Phil commented that it was the first visible change to our workplace in years, and although they could have used spreadsheets, I loved how, on Monday morning, I got a sense of how things were going just by walking around the office.

So things were going well, which made me happy.

Later that evening, though, I got a nasty surprise in the form of a sensible question. A strangely technical email query from Eleanor.

Steve-
How on FPP do you really know that your software really is GETS, considering you haven't shipped anything yet?
Curious.
Perhaps Ron can help?
E

Ten seconds later I was on my way to Ron McKnight's office. As much as it pained me, I needed help from the old man.

CHAPTER FIFTY-ONE

I stood outside Ron's office at the opposite corner of the building. It was 8:36 p.m.

I took a deep breath, knocked, then pushed the door open.

Ron sat there at his desk, typing in the dark, his face lit up in dull green by the reflection from his screen. Green meant he was looking at old mainframe code. Without bothering to look up, he mumbled, "Just a moment," and kept on typing. As I waited, I looked at his desk, which was stacked high with books and papers. Wyx-Fin Group's clear-desk policy was one of many rules that didn't apply to Ron.

When he finally looked up, he had a smile on his face, but that dropped away when he saw it was me.

"Steven."

"Nice to see you too, Ron."

"You've come about the FPP review."

"Review?"

"Oh ... didn't Eleanor tell you?" He smiled, and I thought, looked pleased with himself.

I shook my head.

"While you were away, she and Norbert asked me to run an independent assessment of FPP's health."

I shrugged. Who could blame them?

"Give me a minute." He clicked a few times and his printer (no one else in the entire building, except Hal's PA, had their own printer) whirred behind him. Its lights flashed as it warmed up and I felt my shoulders tense.

"How about you give me the two-minute version?"

"I'll give you the three-word version instead: they're fine."

Unfortunately, in Scotland the word *fine* can mean anything from *Excellent* to *Okay* to *I'll tell you it's fine, but only because I'm too polite to tell you it's not.* But since Ron was grumpy, opinionated and not the sort to hold back, I nodded and said, "Great. Thanks."

Then I added, "That's two words, not three."

"Technically, 'they're' is two words, Steve."

"Okay." I didn't know if he was right, but he usually was. And when he wasn't … Honestly, it wasn't worth the effort arguing.

The printer ejected a single page and stopped. Ron passed it to me. `For Eleanor Scharlau and Norbert Billings` was written at the top.

"Read it. I think you'll be pleasantly surprised."

Ron and I didn't always get along so well, but I valued his opinion far more than I thought he valued mine. He wasn't a bad old guy, just worn down by the years, I guess.

I jumped directly to the last paragraph, which is where the gotchas normally hide.

```
I, the author, have only one concern: In order for in-
cremental development to work, each increment must be
good enough to ship. I have seen no proof, as of yet,
that this is indeed the case on FPP. Who knows what
trolls lie under the bridge until we look under said
bridge?
```

I said, "Trolls?"

He scowled. "Read the whole thing first."

My jaw dropped when I read the first paragraph:

```
FPP's approach to delivering software (the so-called
"inverted pyramid" approach), is merely a variation on
well-established incremental delivery methods, which
have been used by considerably larger software develop-
ment projects for decades.
```

"Incremental delivery methods"?

He nodded.

"What do you mean by the word incremental?"

"At the start of a project, you prioritize your features, then deliver them in chunks of code which are fully tested and—to use your term—good enough to ship. Each chunk is an increment, though some people also refer to an increment as the period of time taken to build the increment. Sound familiar?"

I nodded reluctantly. "But ... that means my inverted pyramid approach ... it already exists?"

"That should be clear, given my choice of words."

"I thought, well ... I thought I'd, like ... I'd invented it."

He laughed, but I couldn't tell if he meant it in a friendly kind of way or if he was mocking me. "You inverted the pyramid, but you didn't invent it. You rediscovered it. And renamed it. It's just a shame you didn't think to do it at the start of FPP, rather than after you'd built all that code, but otherwise, you did well."

I crossed my arms. "Are you sure about this?"

He didn't react initially, but then he smiled in a way that made me uneasy. He said, "You want proof, lift my monitor."

I scrunched my face up in a "huh?" expression.

He gestured toward his desk. I looked there for a large lizard. It must have been hiding, because I couldn't see it.

"Come on. Lift it." He pointed at his computer screen. "I need one of the books boosting it."

I lifted the monitor and he pulled a thick, bluc book from the top of the pile.

I put the monitor back in its place as Ron wiped the layer of dust from the book's cover.

I read the title out loud. *Software Engineering Economics*. It was by Barry Boehm. I knew of the book and the author. Both had been influential in the 70s and 80s, the early years of commercial software development.

"That's the book with the original cost of change curve, right?"

He raised his eyebrows. "I'm surprised you knew that."

He opened the book and thumbed through the pages until he found the one he was looking for.

"Page forty-one," he said. He stabbed the page on the heading 4.4 Refinements of the Waterfall Development, then pulled his finger down the page until it rested below a sub-heading near the bottom. Incremental Development.

He turned the book to face me and I read the first paragraph: *Incremental development should develop software in increments of functional capability.*

Ron flipped to the next page and we continued reading side by side.

Boehm described incremental development as a refinement of the waterfall mode, whereby much of the planning, analysis and design was done up front, but the functionality was built and tested in increments. One of its advantages, he wrote, was that functional increments were much more helpful and easier to test than intermediate-level components. Another advantage is that they provided a cheaper way to include user experience feedback into the product, earlier.

Incremental Development had been successfully used on what Boehm described as extremely large projects (one which cost over a hundred million dollars, way back in the 70s) as well as small projects. I found that last bit about smaller projects particularly interesting. I could easily see how an eighteen-month project could be chopped up into three six-month increments or six three-month increments. I could also easily imagine delivering a six-month project as three two-month increments. In those cases, an increment was just a smaller project—a smaller batch. I found it harder, though, to imagine how a two-month project could be broken down into four or eight smaller chunks.

Thankfully, Boehm gave a simple example of a small incremental project for a software estimation package. The first increment delivered basic functionality: bulk input, some calculations, simple printout. The second built upon the first increment, adding the ability to save and retrieve previous runs and to modify data. The third increment added optional but useful features, like schedule calculations and activity breakdowns.

I pointed at the book, "This is interesting, but right now I'm worried. I need your help. How do I know if our software is truly GETS?"

"When did Boehm know his estimation software was truly GETS?"

There really was only one answer. "After they launched their first increment?"

He nodded, and after ten minutes of work around his whiteboard we had a solution. We would ship FPP into our live environments immediately. If things went smoothly, then good; if not, then even better; we'd found problems and we could fix them while we still had runway ahead of us.

Once we'd shipped we would be live, from an engineering perspective, and Catherine's team could set up their first few live test accounts to kick the tires, but they wouldn't do much more than that. And, since we were live, we would have to switch into S and M mode, using Ron's teams' processes to make small, incremental updates to our production software.

It sounded easy, but neither of us expected it to be.

I stood back and studied Ron's whiteboard, satisfied but annoyed with myself. "I should have thought to do this earlier."

He shook his head solemnly. "Wrong. You should have asked for help earlier."

Tuesday, October 17th
FPP launch date - December 1st, this year

CHAPTER FIFTY-TWO

The following morning, Phil and I met with the manager of our local operations team and one of her senior guys to figure out how to actually ship rather than just potentially ship. Ninety minutes later, as I showed them out of my office after a fraught meeting, I heard Catherine call my name. I looked up and saw her marching toward me, a determined look on her face. She'd been waiting for our meeting to finish.

I hadn't seen much of her during the previous few weeks, partly because I had been on vacation but also because she'd relocated to her new call center office across town where she was forming FPP's operational team.

Gregor was a few steps behind her. He didn't look happy. It looked like I was about to play referee again.

I gestured them in and they sat, both with their arms firmly crossed. I wheeled my desk chair over and joined them.

"Shoot," I said, to Catherine.

Gregor's hands flew out in front of him. "Catherine wants to—"

Catherine threw her hand up like an old-fashioned cop making a stop sign gesture. "Give me a moment. Will you? You are so impatient."

He glared at her then looked across at me, hoping I'd intervene. I didn't know what was going on, so I made that shoulder shrugging gesture that says, *I'm on your side, but give her a moment, will you.*

He tightened his mouth and returned that raised-eyebrow gesture that says, *Okay, you're the boss, but you're not going to like this.* Then he folded his arms, leaned back in his chair and let Catherine speak.

Or at least, that's how I interpreted things. Maybe he'd just had a bad kebab the night before.

Catherine squirmed in her chair. "Mark and I want to launch FPP with basic web app functionality. Okay?"

I shook my head emphatically. "No way. Noooo way. We cannot risk undoing all the good work we've just done getting FPP on track."

She said, "Hear me out, okay? We only need a small web app for our December 1st release. Just enough so we can honestly add to our marketing copy that we have one. We don't need the full web app we descoped back in August. Customers can log in, check their balances and transactions—those basic sorts of things. We can add more features between December and April, if we need to. Okay?"

I said, "Not really."

I looked at Gregor and raised my eyebrows in that way that says *I see what you mean ...*

She leaned forward and spoke in a hushed voice. "Don't get angry with me, okay? But I spoke to Ron and he said it would be easier than we think."

What's the first thing you do when someone tells you not to get angry? "Catherine!" I blurted. "You went behind my back?"

"He said that adding simple web app functionality back on should be relatively easy. He said a new team could work on it, mostly, without interrupting the other FPP work by"—she looked at her notes, then made finger quotes—"*by reusing the existing services and code.* Whatever that means."

I nodded. Ron was right, technically speaking, but technically speaking wasn't good enough. Technically speaking, I could pierce my nipples, if I wanted to, but I didn't want to and so I wouldn't.

Gregor took his chance to speak. "Yeah, but like I said, Catherine, no matter what Ron says, it's still a decent sized project in its own right, with a considerable amount of uncertainty. Projects like that have habits of growing arms and legs."

She held up her hand again. "I haven't finished yet."

I said, "No. Catherine. I know how much you want this, but I have to say no."

"I was about to say—"

"No Catherine. I am sorry, but no. End of conversation."

Her nostrils flared. Her face tightened and her jaw jutted out and quivered just a bit, as if she was deliberately forcing her mouth to remain closed.

Moments passed.

Then she breathed out slowly and nodded.

"Okay. I give up."

Gregor, happy he had won but looking to smooth things out, said in a soft voice, "You had to ask. You wouldn't be doing your job if you didn't."

"True." Catherine said, "Well, in that case, there is one more thing."

She flipped her laptop open and placed it on the table.

"You recognize this?"

It was Gregor's planning spreadsheet.

"Of course."

Gregor nodded, but I could tell from his face that he had no idea what Catherine was about to do. It was almost like she'd set us up by asking for something she knew she couldn't get, then asking for something else, smaller, in our moment of weakness when we felt guilty for saying no. I narrowed my eyes, watching her next move with suspicion.

She turned the laptop toward herself and away from us so that I couldn't directly see the screen. She typed a bit, clicked a couple of times, and then turned the screen back to face us both.

She'd highlighted a row. It was a new row for a new feature named Customer Level Income. It was at the top of the sheet, and had no numbers in the Estimated Effort cell.

The name customer level income seemed familiar, but I couldn't place it.

She said, "What's stopping me from having this feature?"

She'd never asked to add something to the list before. The answer, I suppose, depended on how much effort it would take and who we'd need to work on it. Adding a new feature to the top of the spreadsheet also meant that other features would get pushed back and some of those further down the priority list would miss the December launch.

I turned to Gregor.

His thick neck had turned crimson. "Due respect and all, Catherine, but we rejected that change request about seventeen times already."

Oh!

This wasn't a new feature; this was a change request. I'd recognized it because Gregor had rejected it in his management meeting, the one where I'd announced Phil's discovery about FPP and our War Room.

I leaned forward, suddenly very eager to see what happened next.

"You did, indeed," she said, with false patience in her voice. "But last night, while thinking about work—sad, I know—I realized that I no longer have to beg for change requests. Instead, I simply have to ask you to ask your staff to estimate how long it will take, and then I prioritize it against the other features we're delivering. So I'd like to know by lunchtime today, if you please, how much effort this will take to ship and whether it puts our December date at risk. That's all."

Her request sounded harmless, but I felt my jaw tighten. It felt like she'd played us, using our inverted pyramid approach as a weapon against us. I stumbled around in my mind, looking for a reason to say no. I couldn't find one.

I looked at Gregor, hoping he had some words of wisdom. He shrugged.

I scowled—a lot of good he was—and looked back to Catherine.

She summed up her argument. "I am not requesting a change, Steve. I'm not even begging for a change. I am simply reprioritizing our list."

I said nothing as her words sunk in. She was right. This was not a change request, this was a reprioritization.

I turned to Gregor. "Can we absorb this and still deliver Catherine's bare minimum?"

"We can absorb this, I guess, but not this *and* the web app."

Catherine sat forward in her chair. "Your bottleneck improvements are working and we're running at easily twice the speed we were a month ago, right?"

Gregor nodded and said, "Probably more." But he didn't look happy.

"So we've got wiggle room. I know that when you add this feature I'll lose some lower priority request from my must-have list.

But I'm willing to make that trade."

I'm quite sure I frowned a bit on the outside, but I also know for sure that on the inside I was smiling. Catherine had just evaporated the underproduction conflict I'd discussed with Craig during the summer.

"Okay. I can't see any logical reason why, Gregor, you can't get Catherine the estimates she needs to decide whether this is viable or not."

Gregor sucked in a sharp breath through what I guessed were clenched teeth. "Okay. I'll have a number for you by the close of business tomorrow."

Catherine smiled sweetly, as if she'd just won a small victory against us.

Or maybe she was just happy, and I was interpreting her smile unfairly because I felt like I'd just given something away. Whatever it was, it felt odd.

She said, "Excellent! But look, I remember what your old estimate was to make this change. Even if the new estimate is five times that, I still want it. Pauline, my ex-friend, left before we came up with our change request, so this will differentiate ours from Chaste's."

Gregor said, "Okay. Unless you hear otherwise from me this afternoon, consider it bumped it up to near the top of list number one."

Catherine stood and we shook hands. She smiled. "Thank you. Thank you, so much. This is awesome news."

CHAPTER FIFTY-THREE

Later that evening, after I'd put the kids to bed and feeling in a positive frame of mind, I returned to the office. Ron had been helping our operations guys prepare to move FPP into our live environment, and a plan had been slowly forming in the back of my mind ever since Catherine's visit earlier in the day. I needed to run it past him.

I poked my head around his office door and knocked.

"Any news on our go live?" I asked.

"Nothing exciting."

"Good." I stepped into his office. "Can you, maybe, help me with a problem, then?"

"Of course."

"Catherine called by my office today. She had two change requests. I approved one of them. I wanted to talk about the other one."

He seemed to redden a bit, embarrassed perhaps that Catherine had spoken to him behind my back.

He said, "The FPP web app?"

I nodded. "You told her that it would be easier than most people think to build an FPP web app."

"I wasn't meaning to step on anyone's—"

I put my hand up. "I've thought about it, and it's a good idea."

"Oh?"

"It's not like this is the first website we've ever built, so can use existing architecture, infrastructure and processes. Plus, we'd call on FPP's existing services, and unless we find problems with those services, there should be little need to modify FPP's code. So, yes, I agree it is relatively easy to do."

"Okay." He still looked suspicious. "So why do you need my help?"

"I want one of your teams to build it. Incrementally. Using your three-list system."

"Incrementally?"

I nodded.

He picked up a pen and started tapping it on his desk. "Which team?"

"Well, it would have to be a team with experienced web developers, right?"

"Of course. And they're all plenty busy."

"So I'd have to find a team that could cancel their existing work easily."

"Easily? Good luck with that."

"I could rely on luck, Ron. Or, I could find a bunch of projects whose sponsor really, really, really wants FPP to succeed. Do you know where I might find someone like that?"

His face lit up and he pushed back in his chair. "Oh, that's clever! Mark cancels some of his own, less important, web projects and then moves the people working on them onto FPP. FPP gets a web app. FPP is more appealing and it sells better. Mark looks good. We look good. Good."

He paused and looked at me as if seeing me for the first time. "They'd need help from an FPP analyst, since my guys have no FPP business knowledge."

"Yes. I was thinking of Krzysztof."

Ron thought a moment. "Yes, I like him."

I said, "And we'd need a list #1. I could do with your help putting that together."

His face opened up into a broad smile. "You want to take a stab at that now?"

It took just over twenty minutes to list and prioritize all the things we thought the new FPP website could do. Ron typed them into a spreadsheet he named FPP Web List #1. Some features—Login, Register and Forgot-Password—came mostly for free because we used our existing infrastructure, but our new team would have to build other features that were specific to FPP. Some features were mandatory, some were vital, some were nice to have. List #1 was like one of those huge, multi-page menus you get in some Chinese restaurants. Our next job was to pick just a few dishes from the entire menu, move them to the top of the list, and then place our first order—what Ron called Drop #1.

Another twenty minutes later we had a draft plan for Drop #1. We figured it would take between three and five weeks from when we started construct until Drop #1 was technically GETS. Drop #1 was like the foundation and ground floor of a tall building. We'd do a lot of work, but since most of it was hidden, we'd have little to show for it: a dashboard with nothing on it apart from the customer's name and account number and a balance. We'd build it so it was technically GETS, but Catherine would have to decide whether it was commercially GETS before we considered going live with it.

We then sketched out how we might add slices of functionality on top of Drop #1 until we had four months' worth of work ahead of us. We were kicking the tires, trying to determine if we could launch FPP in December with a bare bones website that we could then grow, slice by slice, by April. We figured we could, even if we got unlucky. These subsequent drops of features were like adding more floors to our imaginary high-rise, and since they would be built on a solid foundation, we'd make much faster progress than with the first drop.

Just before 10 p.m. I called Mark and suggested that if we cancelled three of his marketing projects, we could build him a bare bones FPP website—one that was good enough to claim truthfully that FPP had a web app, but would then grow as need be over time.

He asked me if I was serious. When I said I was, he offered to name one of his illegitimate children after me, an offer I declined politely. I called Catherine and she asked me if I'd been drinking. It wasn't until Ron took my phone and told her it was true that she believed me.

When Ron had finished his conversation and hung up the phone, I stuck my hand out toward him. He looked at it hanging there, considered it a moment, then reached across and we shook.

As soon as that awkward moment had passed he said, "Do you know what you've just done here?"

I wasn't sure what he meant, so I gave him a few obvious answers to choose from.

"We've just figured out how to build a web app?"

"Yes, but I'm thinking of something far grander, far more significant than that. We build web apps all the time."

"We've just delighted Mark and Catherine."

He shook his head.

"We just made the company more money?"

He shook his head then gave me a hint. "You've inverted something from scratch."

"Oh." I blinked, then repeated his words. "We've just inverted our first project, from scratch."

He smiled and started tidying some papers on his desk. After a minute he said, "That wasn't what I was thinking of. You inverted something far more important than a little web project."

I frowned, but nothing came to me. I looked up again and said, "Hint?"

He shook his head.

What had we done? We'd created a brand new, very important project, but that wasn't it. And in order to do that we'd postponed a few considerably less important projects.

That was it.

"We just inverted our projects list?"

He nodded.

We had three lists of projects: those not yet started, those in progress, and those we'd finished. Mark and I had just moved one project from Project List #1 to Project List #2, and moved three projects from List #2 back to List #1.

I said, "I never thought of it that way."

Ron smiled, and I realized for the first time after years of working with him that hidden under his gruff exterior was a genius. His way of working looked simple, but it was simple by design. That wasn't easy.

I said again, "We've just inverted our projects list."

He nodded. "Not entirely, but you've made a start."

Saturday, October 21st
FPP launch date - December 1st, this year

CHAPTER FIFTY-FOUR

"Norbert, you are *not* listening to me. We have no choice. We *have* to call the vendor's specialists in from Australia. We cannot fix this ourselves."

Phil was speaking—shouting, really—into the video conference camera back in Watt's Bridge.

It was 10 a.m. there and 11 a.m. in Malmö, where I'd called in from my hotel room using my laptop's video conferencing software. Norbert was at home across the bridge in Copenhagen. He'd turned sixty earlier in the week, and I was one of many who'd flown over for the formal Wyxcomb celebrations. He looked a lot healthier than I felt.

On the screen I could see Phil, Gregor and eight of our techies, who looked smelly and tired. Five of them were Watt's Bridge locals and three had been flown in from other European Wyxcomb sites to help us. They were all back in Scotland in the FPP conference room, once again our War Room.

Our infamous messaging system, which had caused us so much trouble when we first inverted FPP, had delayed our first chunk and scared the bejesus out of us. It had been working without hassle on our development environments for weeks, but would not work on our production systems.

FPP wasn't GETS, yet. Our shipment had hit the fan, so to speak. Everything we'd worked on, all the promises we'd made, were in jeopardy.

Why? How? No one knew. Yet.

I added my news. "I've checked, and their specialists can catch a flight from Melbourne today. They'll be tired when they get here but they can start working on the problem tomorrow. Provided they stay off the free booze.

Phil said, "They can stick to the Australian time zone and we'll switch to working nights if we have to."

Norbert said, "Okay. Steve, fly them first class."

"I'm sure we can get business class flights."

"No. We need them as productive as possible when they get to you. And Steve, you need to initiate Plan B today."

I pulled a face. In Plan B we reverted to the old tried-and-tested technology that the messaging system was supposed to replace. CORETRAN used the old technology, and our CORETRAN developers were the only experts in it. Most of those who knew the technology had retired by now, and no younger folk with the brainpower to work on it would learn it because, frankly, that was career suicide. If we went live with the old technology, then all future FPP development would compete with every other CORETRAN request. Our technology strategy was to do the exact opposite, which was why FPP had used the new technology. Plan B sucked.

That said, Ron had figured out that his six best CORETRAN developers could work with FPP's developers and testers to rip the guts of our new messaging system code out of FPP and replace it, and still go live within three to six weeks. That sounded too optimistic to me. So, we might still launch on December 1st, if we started soon, but Ron had made it very clear that we might hit a few quality issues after we went live, given the breadth of the changes. I really didn't like Plan B.

I said, "I think we should give the vendors another week."

I saw Norbert flinch on the screen in front of me. "I did not ask you to consider kicking off Plan B, Steven. It was not a question, it was an instruction. Kick off Plan B, today, without delay." My team on the video feed coming from Watt's Bridge all politely turned away from the screen. Norbert said, "Your only priority is to ship FPP on December 1st. Nothing else matters. Nothing. Do you understand that, Steven?"

"Yes." I blinked. "I'll kick off plan B ASAP."

He shook his head. "Not ASAP. Immediately."

I nodded. "Okay."

He nodded and then hung up.

I thanked the guys in the War Room, suggested they go home and say hello and goodbye to their loved ones, and that we'd talk again at 4 p.m. I asked Phil to hang on a minute.

He waited until the room was clear, then said, "You okay?"

I smiled weakly. "Yeah."

"Norbert's normally Mr. Nice Guy."

"Yeah. Normally."

Phil and I chatted a few minutes, agreeing he'd talk to Ron and together they'd kick off Plan B—immediately—and I'd get the flights from Australia sorted out.

We hung up, and I reached over and picked up my hotel phone. I dialed the vendor's President's number from memory. I didn't know what time it was there. I didn't care.

Monday, October 30th
FPP launch date - December 1st, this year

CHAPTER FIFTY-FIVE

A week later I went to meet Catherine for an "urgent" lunch in Lister square, halfway between Wyx-Fin HQ and her new FPP call center on the other side of the old town.

Lister Square sits smack in the middle of Watt's Bridge. The ornate, stone council chambers, which look foreboding on a grey day and sparkle on a sunny day, sit on one side of the square. A modern shopping mall takes up another side and the city's ancient defensive walls guard another. By royal decree back in the 1900s, the fourth side was left completely clear in perpetuity, providing views out across the city's lower wards and toward the sea.

Lister was an English surgeon who, while working up the road in Glasgow in the 1860s, discovered he could save many of his patients' lives by washing their wounds and his surgical tools with a carbolic acid wash prior to surgery. His practices spread across the world, saving many lives, and he became famous. He had nothing to do with the mouthwash Listerine, but it was named after him.

That seemed to be the way things were done back then. Lord Kelvin developed the concept of absolute zero, in Scotland, and was instrumental in rolling out the trans-Atlantic telegraph. He got a brand of refrigerator named after him. Watt invented the steam engine in Scotland, kicked off the modern world, and got his name plastered across billions of light bulbs around the world. Mr. Steven J. Abernethy invents a way to deliver an impossible project on time, and gets—what? Plan B named after me? Plan Abernethy.

Nice. Not.

I sat down on one of the benches in the middle of the square, near another of Watt's Bridge's tourist attractions: Lister Fountain. I sat facing the sun and the sea and just enjoyed the solitude. I was ready for a little rest.

In the distance, a container ship sat on the horizon, waiting for a tug to come and pull it into port. I yawned. Then, out of the corner of my eye, I saw Catherine step out of the Marks and Spencer store and scan the square. She carried a small Marks and Spencer plastic bag.

I stood and waved.

As soon as she'd sat she pulled a large Caesar Salad roll from the shopping bag and tore the plastic wrapper off. I noticed she had dark rings under her eyes and her hair was tied back in an efficient, but unflattering, ponytail. "How was Madrid?" she said, with a mouthful of roll.

"Barcelona. Though it could easily have been Madrid, or London, or New York. Conference centers look pretty much the same no matter where you are in the world. The lunches in Barcelona were particularly good."

"Poor you, with your first world problems," she said unsympathetically. "If you don't enjoy the traveling, why do you keep doing it?"

I shrugged and changed the subject. "How are you doing?"

She swallowed and scowled. "Steven, my get-up-and-go has not only got up and gone, it's taken my will to live with it."

I deconstructed her sentence while I removed my own sandwich from its bag.

"You look tired," I said, pointing out the obvious.

"No shit, Sherlock. While you've been busy gallivanting around the world telling everyone how great Wyxcomb is and having fancy lunches, I've been working my arse off." She sighed deeply. "How's your messaging system? Still stuck up shipment creek without a paddle?"

I shrugged. "The Australia team is packaging up their latest fix and we'll have it tomorrow morning."

"Odds of this fix working?"

"Honestly? It might work, it might not. But if it doesn't, then we'll just start working on the new problem. And so on. This is how these things work. It's just a matter of time." I didn't tell her about Plan B yet.

She made an "eek" face. "Mark spoke with Hal over the weekend."

"Oh?"

"Hal wants us live, on December 1st, whether your software is ready to launch or not. We will go live with a paper and spreadsheet solution, if we have to, and key everything into the system when it's fixed. This, Hal says, is an acceptable business risk, considering the tiny sales volume."

I shook my head slowly, not liking it, but then I nodded. "Realistically, I don't think we'll need to do that. We still have a month to go."

"But you can't be sure."

I shook my head.

"Okay. Now, I need your help." Her face darkened. "I am drowning, Steve. And, just so you know, it's your stupid fault."

I blinked. What now?

"No one ever expected you to launch your software on time, Steve. And if Mark and I had known you would pull off your little miracle then we would have started our rollout work much sooner."

She stopped and looked at me, checking my reaction.

"I understand that."

"But now, you not only look quite the hero, but all that pressure you were under—it hasn't gone. It's just slid down off your shoulders and landed on mine."

She then listed off her problems on her fingers. "One. We've got our internal launch event on the 17th. And, Mark being Mark, he insists on putting on a big fancy show. An event is how he put it. He's invited everyone of any importance—plus you, by the way. And he's written me into the script. And you. You better dust off your best suit."

I raised my eyebrows wondering what part I'd play in his little show.

"Two. My team is mad busy creating the training material for our branches and the call center and— three—I'm figuring out how to roll the training out, once it's finished, to all thirty-six Scottish branches during—I hope—the last two weeks of November, something which, frankly, is—" she checked I was keeping up, "impossible."

"Impossible?"

She nodded. "On top of all that— four— we've got the ramp up of the call center: the installation of the equipment, the recruitment, the training, and so on and so on. And, of course, that task is bigger and harder than we ever expected since I deprioritized a lot of automation work so that you could deliver on time. And, while all this is going on—five—I'm still steering your team's development effort."

I said an ambiguous okay, unsure whether I was being blamed for this or if she was just letting off steam.

"Look," she said, clenching her hands, her roll forgotten for now. "Bottom line is, our ramp up and rollout is far from being a certainty. Unless I do something drastic, it's very unlikely we'll be ready to go live on December 1st."

"You are kidding me?"

"Look at me. Do I look like I'm kidding?"

I looked at her and decided she most certainly did not.

"Why didn't you say anything until now?" She'd had a month to figure this out.

She looked down at her hands, then slowly up again. "I've been swamped ramping up our ramp up and ... I never had time to sit down and figure out if it were feasible."

I nodded sympathetically. I'd been in that same place—too overwhelmed to plan—just a few weeks ago.

Then Catherine smiled awkwardly, as if she were embarrassed. "You know, I feel awful saying this, but over the weekend, as the situation became clearer, I almost found myself hoping your messaging system problem doesn't get fixed, so you get blamed for us shipping late and not me."

I raised an eyebrow.

"I said almost." She shrugged. "I spent all Sunday with Mark, at his estate. We have a plan, but we need your help."

"Go ahead"

"We are in this together, you and me, right?"

"Of course," I said eyeing her suspiciously.

"Good. There are two bits to my plan, and the first bit has a big impact on your development team. I need more people working on the rollout."

"Let me guess. You want to borrow some of my FPP staff to help you with your ramp-up?" I smiled to show I wasn't entirely opposed to the idea.

She shook her head. "No, actually, I don't. I need to move half of my business analysts off your development work onto my rollout."

A chill crawled down my back. "That's worse! My bottleneck will move. Our developers and testers will become starved of work."

"Maybe, maybe not. At the moment, most of the BAs aren't just doing BA work. They spend over half their time helping with testing. I doubt your bottleneck will move, but it might intensify. But, whatever. Honestly, I don't care."

"Don't care?" I said. "If you cut our bottleneck capacity the entire team slows down."

"The entire *development* team, but that's not our concern now." She shrugged. "I've done some thinking and—you're not going to like this—if we were desperate, we could go live with the GETS features we already have under our belts."

The chill changed to heat and crept to my face. Hadn't we already slashed the product back to its barest bones? "How is that possible?" I stammered.

"Last night, I took a red pen to our call center scripts and pared them back enough that we could go live today with what we've got. Don't get me wrong. I don't want to go live today, but we could if we had to."

Unbelievable. Her bare minimum, her slam dunk scope, had shrunk yet again. "It would have been nice of you to let us know that earlier," I said.

"I didn't know earlier, and besides, I'm still learning to work this new way. I've never had a genuine phase two before."

I studied her face and I realized that I was being hard on her. We were all learning.

"Fair enough," I said.

I closed my eyes a moment and cleared my head. "Let me summarize. One, Hal is willing to go live with a paper and spreadsheet solution if our messaging system isn't live on December 1st. Two, you've slashed your slam dunk scope back even further. Three, you'll pull half your BAs from the development work, and four, Gregor and Tim will figure out how to adapt."

"There's one more thing. It's a biggie for us, not so big for you."

That's what she thought.

It turned out to be enormous.

CHAPTER FIFTY-SIX

"So what's this other thing?"

"Consider the facts. Our launch date is fixed in stone and it's very unlikely we've got enough time to rollout to all of our branches. What do we do, if that date is truly fixed?"

"Well, you either add capacity, which you've already done, or you flex your scope."

She half-smiled, half-grimaced. "I need to invert my branch list then rollout to the branches incrementally."

I stared at her. It seemed I wasn't the only genius on the bench.

"Mark and I want to launch in only one branch, the Watt's Bridge branch, on December 1st, then rollout to the other branches after that. The alternative is that we go live badly in thirty-six branches, and although we might look good for a few weeks, we'll soon look like idiots.

"There's a problem though." She twisted her head to one side and closed one eye so that she looked like a thrush listening for worms. "You looked like a hero when you inverted FPP's feature list. But me, if I do the same with our branch rollout, I'll just look like the clumsy oaf who dropped the ball right in front of the goal. Hal would eat Mark and me for breakfast. And I don't want that."

I sensed where she was going with this.

"So, I need your help to help me wrap a ribbon around this

pig."

"Wrap a what around a what?"

"It's one of Mark's sayings. A pig is just a pig until you put a ribbon on it; then it becomes a gift. It means we need to turn this pig of a situation into a gift for Hal by wrapping a ribbon around it."

"Cute. How, exactly, do you intend doing that?"

"First, let me share an example Mark gave me. A few years ago, Mark bought a new router for his house that had a feature splashed all over the front of the box called "Automatic Network Healing." You know him, he's a bit of a gadget man, and he thought it sounded cool. He said his old router got its knickers in a twist every few weeks and he had to reboot the damned thing to fix it, so he liked the idea of a router that healed itself automatically.

"Now, I'm hardly the most technical of people, Steve, so let me ask you this: Do you know how the Automatic Network Healing feature worked?"

I shook my head.

"Mark said he read the instructions, and if you switch the feature on, then the router reboots itself, automatically, at 3 a.m. every morning."

It took a moment for the brilliance of the solution to sink in. That wasn't the work of a developer. That was the work of a marketer. Or a psychopath.

"He was duped!"

"That's one way of looking at it, but look at what they did. They took the pig—their flaky software—and turned it into a gift: a router that does actually perform better."

"Hmm. And you want to do the same with our pig? How do we do that?"

She smiled. "Mark and I already have a plan."

"I figured," I said, realizing that nothing in this conversation had happened by chance.

"You're not going to believe what we came up with."

"Try me."

And she did.

Basically, they'd taken the positive aspects of our pig—that we would only launch in one branch and that our product was much smaller than we'd ever intended—and they'd wrapped a ribbon around it by figuring out how to both amplify the positives and address the negatives until they had what Hal would hopefully call a bloody good idea.

It reminded me of what Craig had done with Wyx-Health.

"So, what you're saying is that, if we had a time machine and could roll back to the start of FPP, then we should have started with a tiny product which we launched in just one branch?"

She blanked for a moment, as if she'd not thought of it that way. "Actually, yes."

"What do you need from me?"

She answered in one breath. "I want a dedicated FPP sub team primed and ready, like a Formula One pit crew, to action change requests as quickly as they can based on what we learn from launching in the branch."

I nodded. "Okay. A change request team. That's easy enough. Is that it?"

"Yes. And it'd be nice if you could get that messaging system fixed, too."

I nodded and then shook my head. I looked at my watch. I really should be heading back. I shook my head, again.

Maybe it was because I shook my head twice, rather than just the one time. Whatever it was, something rattled around inside my brain. Connections were made. New neurothingies grew. And a crazy idea began forming inside my head.

I needed to check something. "Look, if our messaging system bug didn't get fixed until, say, January, could you cope with your manual systems?"

Her eyes widened in alarm. "For real or hypothetically?"

"Both. It's an unlikely scenario, but we need to consider it."

She shrugged. "I hope it's just your imagination being remarkably negative. We'd build up a pile of paper applications, but we'd cope. We only have one branch to start with, remember. If the product turned out to be popular then we'd just stop the branch staff promoting it until we were ready."

I smiled. "That's what I thought. In that case, we cannot launch on December 1st. There's too much at stake. It's madness."

"What?"

It took a good bit of explaining, but it turned out I'd just taken our pig and done more than wrap ribbons around it. I'd also shoved an apple in its mouth and turned it into the centerpiece of a banquet.

Friday, November 17th
FPP launch date - December 1st, this year

CHAPTER FIFTY-SEVEN

Two weeks later, on Friday the 17th of November, we launched FPP internally, in the basement auditorium of Watt's Bridge HQ. Eleanor and I sat in the back row.

We started with darkness.

And silence.

Then the boom of one hundred Irish tap shoes thundered out over the auditorium's sound system.

Tikatakaitikataktic. Tikatakaitikataktic. Tikatakaitikataktic,

It was from Riverdance. I learned that during rehearsals.

Tikatakaitikataktic, tikatakaitikataktic, tikatakaitikataktic, tikatakaitikataktic, tikatakaitikataktic, tikatakaitikataktic, tikatakaitikataktic, tikatakaitikataktic, tikatakaitikataktic, tikatakaitikataktic, tikatakaitikataktic.

Then silence again.

Then light.

Just one light.

From the back row of the auditorium, I watched the spotlight pierce the darkness and highlight Mark Richmond, Wyx-Fin's chief marketing officer and showman, standing at the front of the stage. He wore a top hat and tails and gripped a megaphone in his hands, holding it out in front of him like James Bond with a pistol.

He leaned into the megaphone. "Ladies and Gentlemen, I present to you—Future Perfect."

Mark dropped the hand holding the megaphone to his side,

then twisted his body to his right and pointed his other hand toward the projection screen. From the distance, I could just make out the faint outline of the screen as it reflected light from the spotlight.

The spotlight switched off and the screen filled with a colorful photograph of a large family gathering. Gentle music played in the background. The photo suddenly burst into life to reveal an eightieth birthday party. An old man sat in an old wooden chair, his whole family—his wife, children, grandchildren, maybe even a great-grandchild—singing "Happy Birthday." His wife held his hand and the man looked very happy.

The camera zoomed in on the elderly couple's faces, the singing faded away, and suddenly their faces lost fifteen years. The camera zoomed out to reveal a retirement party with the same wife and kids, though younger and with fewer grandchildren and no great-grandchildren. The camera zoomed again and the process repeated three more times, with the couple losing a decade or so each time until we saw the same couple, now in their thirties, with an infant child bouncing on the mother's lap. They beamed with obvious joy at a very pretty Wyx-Fin saleswoman.

The wife, who held the Wyx-Fin application form clearly in view, turned to her husband and said, "We're in safe hands, darling." The picture froze and morphed into a photograph. A deep and reassuring male voice ended the segment: "Wyxcomb Financials' Future Perfect, for your perfect future."

Cheesy? Oh yes. But they worked. The Wyx-Fin family series of adverts had been at the center of Wyx-Fin's advertising strategy for the last half dozen years because, as cheesy as they were, they pulled customers into our retail branches and made us buckets of money.

The spotlight came on and highlighted Mark once again, the megaphone gone now. Theatrically, he rolled up his sleeves, and like a magician proving he had nothing to hide, he held out his fists and slowly opened them palms-up, proving to any cynics in the audience that they were indeed empty. Then he sprang into the air and seemingly snatched the application form straight out of the photograph on the screen. He landed and smiled broadly, waving a real application form at the audience.

Like I said, cheesy.

The overhead lights came on. Mark stepped down off the stage and walked to the front row until he stood in front of Catherine. He bowed to her, then handed her the application form. She accepted it gracefully, with a small nod.

The audience erupted in applause.

All except for Hal.

I watched him intently from my vantage point in the back row. He knew what was about to happen, but he'd been clear in rehearsals that he didn't approve of theatrics. As soon as the applause died down, he stuck his hand up as if he were a schoolboy seeking permission to ask a question. This wasn't part of our script.

Mark, though momentarily thrown, kept smiling. "Hal?"

"Smoke and mirrors?" spat Hal. "Is that all you've got? Smoke and mirrors?"

Mark's a pro, though, and he didn't lose his cool.

"No sir," he said, with what I knew to be mock respect. Then he turned to the audience, his smile looking a bit forced now. "Enough with the sizzle. Let's talk about the steak."

Mark quickly bought everyone up to speed about FPP's history and future and then handed the microphone over to Catherine, who quickly described FPP's back office setup. She clicked on her laptop and its screen appeared on the overhead screen, showing the FPP software we'd spent so many months building.

She held the application form Mark had given her for everyone to see, then opened it and gasped in feigned surprise. "Is there a Mr. Steven J. Abernethy in the room?"

"Up here," I said, waving. The audience spun toward me then back to Catherine.

Catherine laid the application form on the table in front of her and quickly keyed my details into the software, explaining some of the special features of the software as she went. The audience let out a quiet murmur of appreciation when she demonstrated the customer level income feature, explaining how Chaste's product definitely did *not* have this feature.

She finished keying the application, clicked the submit button and asked me to join her. As I made my way toward her, she opened up the laptop's browser and navigated to FPP's custom login page.

She handed me a large hat with the words "S. Abernethy, Customer" on it, and I put it on. I typed my user ID and password, quickly clicked through the few options that were available to me and stepped back from the PC. There wasn't an awful lot to see, really, but the point was that there was *something* to see, and all of our colleagues were seeing that something.

"Thank you, Steven," Catherine said, dismissing me, and I slipped back to my seat.

Catherine looked down at the screen and chuckled. "Typical IT guy. You forgot to log out, Steve."

The audience laughed and Catherine logged me out.

That wasn't rehearsed. I was more nervous than I had realized.

She looked out toward the audience and asked, "Are there any questions?"

There was silence, as always, so Mark jumped in with the first question. "I have a question for you, Catherine."

But Hal interrupted. "Hang on, Mark. I've got a question, for your customer Abernethy at the back of the room."

My heart jumped into my throat.

"I think everyone here would like you to confirm, Steve, that there will be no technical hitches when we go live on December 1st?"

I was surprised at the contempt in Hal's voice, especially since he knew the answer. I was even more surprised when sixty-plus very important heads spun to face me, many of them frowning—recalling messy launches from the past, no doubt.

Mark, Catherine, and I had practiced the answer to this question, but the question wasn't supposed to come from Hal. It was supposed to come from Mark. Hal had forced us to jump ahead a page or so in our script.

I nodded thoughtfully. This was our moment. Time to unveil our first gift-wrapped pig.

I choked. My heart was still in my mouth, and it seemed to be blocking my tongue.

Catherine jumped in to save me, "Let me answer that, Halifax," she said, and the heads spun back to the front of the room to face her.

"Mr. Steve Abernethy is in fact our seventeenth live customer. *Live*." She waited a moment to let that sink in. "After seeking the appropriate independent advice last week, Steve filled out the FPP application form while in our Watt's Bridge High Street branch, and I've just keyed his real, live application into our real, live system."

[The messaging system fix had come through the previous week, and we'd been running FPP live in production since then.]

Catherine paused. "What you've seen was not a demonstration. It was very, very real."

The heads turned back slowly to face me. It was obvious, judging by their expressions, most still didn't understand.

My heart had crept back down in its proper place, and I spoke loudly. "I make my first payment—of real money—on the 21st of November."

Still nothing.

Mark stood up, lifted his megaphone, and shouted, "FPP is alive and kicking two weeks ahead of schedule!"

It took about five seconds for his words to sink in, and then the room let out a collective gasp of approval and started clapping.

Eleanor, our ninth customer, jabbed me with her elbow. I turned to her, and she mouthed the word *nice* to me.

I whispered back to her, "I think so."

"And ..." Mark said, giving the audience time to turn back to him, "a selection of our other Scottish branches will start selling Future Perfect in early January, three months ahead of our original schedule."

An appreciative murmur rose across the auditorium.

Marked continued, "Once those branches are bedded in, we will rollout to our other branches. Our major U.K. branches will be selling FPP by the new financial year."

Mark took a step back and stretched his body to full height.

"Ladies and Gentlemen," he cheered, raising his hands as he did so. "FPP is live!"

CHAPTER FIFTY-EIGHT

Hal waited for the applause to die down before he cut Mark off at the knees.

"Why this timid drip-drip-drip rollout? What are you afraid of, Mark?"

If someone in the audience had a pin and they decided to drop it, then you would almost certainly have heard it drop. Hal seemed genuinely surprised and angry, as if he didn't know about the incremental rollout. I had assumed Mark had filled Hal in, but apparently not. It looked like Mark had decided to seek forgiveness rather than permission. Either that or Hal was a very good actor.

Mark's smile fell and a frown rolled down to take its place. His face hardened. He pulled his hands up in front of him to chest level, joined his fingers to form a steeple, and placed his index fingers against his lips. The entertainer had left the building; the thinker had taken his place. He extended his hands, still steepled, out toward Hal in the unmistakable shape of a revolver.

"An excellent question, Hal." He nodded toward Catherine then smiled graciously. "There are two excellent reasons, which my colleague Catherine will now explain."

Catherine took Mark's place at the lectern and fired up a presentation. We had, apparently, returned to the script.

The first slide showed a picture of a chubby toddler supporting himself with his hand holding on to the front edge of a couch. In nice contrast to the earlier parts of the presentation, which had been professionally constructed by Mark's media team, this photo was obviously an amateur snapshot.

"This is my nephew, Hamish. He's about eighteen months old in this photo, and at that stage between crawling and walking. Not many weeks later, though, he was walking. And not long after that, running."

She paused for effect, and then words appeared under Hamish's picture.

WALK BEFORE YOU RUN.

"We chose to rollout incrementally, in a safe, prudent and focused manner, starting with our local Watt's Bridge branches. They're close by and we already have excellent relationships with the staff. In return for getting a head start selling Wyx-Fin's hottest new product, the local branch will help shape our sales approach, our processes and training material. Like wee Hamish, we are learning to walk so that when we need to run, in April, we can."

She spent another minute explaining how this would work, carefully forgetting to mention that the process and training documentation hadn't been written yet.

She clicked and Hamish faded away. He was replaced with a stock photograph of a racing team pit crew busy changing tires.

"The second advantage of our incremental rollout—and this I believe is truly innovative, something that the entire Wyxcomb Group and perhaps even Chaste Financials will one day emulate—is that although our product is already live, we've not yet finished developing it."

She paused deliberately, giving the audience time to think. How could we be live when the product wasn't finished yet?

"We're using the staggered rollout to test our real, live product with real, live staff and real, live customers. We want to see who buys the product and who doesn't, why they do and why they don't."

She glanced at Mark and he added, "There's nothing like the sound of cash registers ringing to confirm that your customers want your product."

Catherine continued. "When we find something we don't like, something we could do better, then we fix it. If it's process related, we will fix the process. If it's sales related, we'll fix the sales process; and if it needs software changes then Steve's team is primed—like the pit crew you see on the screen behind us—and ready to pounce on any changes we request and implement them immediately.

"And when is the best time for us as a business to learn and adapt like this? When it's easy and cheap, with minimum impact to staff and customers. And when specifically is that? When we have our dedicated IT pit crew standing by and when we only have a few branches up and running with only a few live customers."

And, I thought, when the product is so small it's easy to change.

Catherine stepped aside and Mark took her place.

He looked directly at Hal, but spoke as if addressing the entire audience. "We've got a great product, folks, but we'll keep making it better by listening to our customers' feedback and listening for the cash registers' rings. Every new product launch is a bet, and FPP is, for us, a bigger bet than most. This staggered rollout loads the dice in our favor."

Mark stopped talking and stood there, staring directly at Hal and challenging him to say something nice.

Moments passed.

Then, finally, Hal stood up. He turned to face the entire room. He nodded to Mark and Catherine, then looked up, found me in the back row, and nodded once more.

He pivoted back to face Mark.

"Your team has done excellent work. Though, frankly," he said, before turning and speaking directly to me, "your website is pig-ugly. Not your finest hour, Steven."

I smiled. Pig-ugly was an apt description, and if that was the worst he could say then that was a victory. Four weeks earlier we didn't even have a web app. In two weeks' time the site would look a little prettier. Come March, who knew what it would look like?

I looked around the audience and beamed. Few of them knew what the FPP team had achieved. None knew that I would soon rollout the lessons we'd learned rescuing FPP to other, new Wyx-Fin projects. Not to rescue them, but to set them up to succeed. That was my little secret.

Professionally speaking, I'd never felt more proud or fulfilled in my life as I did at that moment, and I wasn't going to let Hal's comment bother me.

I said, "Thank you, Hal. We are very proud of what we've achieved."

He nodded, then said, "Right, back to work everyone, then."

As the crowd slowly dispersed, Eleanor rested her hand on my lower arm, indicating I should wait with her.

CHAPTER FIFTY-NINE

Eleanor pulled out her mobile, glanced at the screen and said, "Halifax will join us shortly." She then promptly ignored me and used the spare time to process her emails.

I looked at my watch. I had promised to call Norbert the moment we finished. Did I have time to make the call? He said it wouldn't take long, but I decided to wait until Eleanor, Hal and I had caught up.

Mark had laid out celebration drinks and snacks in the cafeteria next door. Later that evening, the entire FPP project team—the folk who had actually done the work—were heading to the Watt's Bridge Castle conference center for a celebration dinner, and then, for the young and young at heart, a disco.

Once the room had emptied, Hal hopped out of his front row seat and marched up the central aisle steps towards Eleanor and me. He swung himself into the seat beside me. For a man his age he was surprisingly agile.

We shook hands. "That went far better than I expected," he said.

"Gee, thanks."

He lowered his voice. "Norbert is telling everyone in Group you're a superhero and inverting is your secret weapon. I've asked my mother to knit you a Christmas jumper with a great big red I on the front."

I smiled politely. He had a caustic way of saying thank you. "And you, Hal? What do you think?"

His eyes narrowed. "You got lucky. Lucky to be managing the wrong project at the right time. Lucky to be working for two tough bosses. One who forced you into an impossible situation and one who forced you to talk to that Lally fellow who then helped you dig yourself out of that situation."

I blanched.

"You asked." He shrugged. "To be fair, you did perform well under pressure."

That was when the tennis match started. Eleanor and Hal were the players, one sitting either side of me, and I was the ball spinning backwards and forwards, left then right, as they talked.

Eleanor served first. "Actually, Steven,"—she gave me time to turn—"that is Hal's way of saying thank you. We both agree you did a splendid job. And ..." she said, leaning forward and glaring at Hal, "Hal and I have a favor to ask of you."

Hal said, "I have some new information for you, then you have a choice to make."

I turned to face Hal. "Choice?"

He surveyed the room, checking no one could overhear our conversation. "You can't repeat what I'm about to tell you. Understand?"

I nodded.

"Let's start with what you already know. One, we made a huge bet when we invested in Future Perfect. Two, it is supposed to resuscitate Wyx-Fin. Three, it might still do that, though we can't know how well it will sell until the new financial year.

"Now, here's what you do not know: When Group agreed to this bet, they made it clear that if the new Future Perfect product is not a significant commercial success, then we will get sold to the highest bidder."

"I see." Although I wasn't privy to the details, I wasn't surprised.

"So, when Chaste came along they blew our business case out of the water. My bosses, figuring their bet was bust, wanted to put Wyx-Fin up on the chopping block. I persuaded them to make another, smaller, but equally important bet."

I said, "You bet we could deliver the FPP project impossibly early."

He nodded.

I smiled, though I was worried about where the conversation was heading. "That bet, at least, seems to have paid off."

He did not return my smile. "Correct. We are not currently on the auction block. But, to be clear, the bigger bet has not yet paid off. If Future Perfect does not sell exceptionally well between April and August next year, then Wyx-Fin still gets sold. You understand?'

I sucked in a sharp breath and held it as I absorbed this new information.

If Wyx-Fin was sold, it would probably be to a competitor. They'd pay more than a non-competitor because they could eliminate a lot of duplicated infrastructure and staff costs. I'd be out of a job almost immediately, and over time so would be most of my staff. Hal and Eleanor would leave the company with a cloud of failure sitting over them.

That wasn't good for us as individuals, but it made business sense. The Group purchased subsidiaries like ours as investments. If they could make more money selling us and investing the money elsewhere than they could by keeping us and reaping the ongoing profits, then that's what they had to do.

Then I recalled my Kelvin's Peak phone conversation with Eleanor, when I had told her FPP would ship by December 1st. I turned to face her. "But what about the four million pounds extra profit you forecast Future Perfect will bring in?"

She said, "The extra cash is nice, but it's a one off, an unexpected bonus. Without it we'd have been sold by now, but in order to truly prevent the sale, Future Perfect must be a significant commercial success. That four million pounds we talked about was based on a very pessimistic forecast. Future perfect needs to sell much better than that."

"And that's why we are talking now," Hal said. "Our business case assumed a much bigger product with many, many more features than you were able to deliver. Plus, of course, we have an aggressive and popular competitor. We expect sales to be much lower than we hoped.

"Worse, if Future Perfect actually does sell well, our administration costs will be much higher than expected. The web app was supposed to allow our customers to do much of their own administration work, to self-serve, but your web app is tiny. That means Catherine's call center and back office will need to be much bigger to cope with the extra administration. On top of that, you descoped most of our back office automation, so their work will be very costly and time consuming. Our future is far from perfect, Steve."

Eleanor said, "But, as grim as that sounds, Future Perfect is live and the FPP team is working to fill the gaps in the product. Thankfully, your defect rate is extremely low, so they will spend their time making genuine improvements rather than fixing bugs. So there are some positives."

I said, "Nine months is a surprisingly long time."

"Exactly. Less than four months have passed since we stumbled upon Chaste's plan. Your new way of working is new to us; we don't know how to work this way yet, but we are looking forward to finding out. Who knows what miracles you and your team can pull off between now and August ..."

She left her question hanging there, as if I was supposed to answer it. So I did. "Especially, if we change our goals from delivering FPP by a fixed date to making Future Perfect financially successful."

Hal cleared his throat. "Which brings us to your choice."

"My choice?"

He nodded towards Eleanor. "You tell him. Technically he works for you, not me."

She sighed. "You see, Steven, now that FPP is now live, Norbert wants you, come January, to work full-time for him in a new job, helping others across the group invert their projects. Initially you'll be rescuing the most important in-flight projects, and then later figuring out how to invert new projects from the start. It will require more travel, but you seem to like that."

My mouth fell open. Apart from the travel, that sounded like the job of my dreams. She'd just described a very high-profile role, which not only would have visibility across the group, but also the potential to have a real and positive impact. It wasn't the job I'd been aspiring to all these years—it was better than that. Where was the choice in that?

"We'd prefer you stay," Eleanor said, and her serious tone made me wary.

"Well, I can see that ..."

Eleanor said, "HR informs me that I cannot force you to stay, but Norbert won't force you to take the job either, since you have a young family. The transfer is not mandatory."

That was when Hal started his sales job. "You shouldn't think of staying as just helping Future Perfect." He shook his head. "Think of it as possibly preventing the sale of the company, and more importantly, saving your staff and your friends' jobs. We are the only major employer of computer people in Watt's Bridge.

"And, also, it's not really a choice. We'd just like you to delay accepting that new job until August next year. You'll have a better story to tell by then, anyway. Hopefully." He shrugged, as if he didn't care, though he clearly did. "The choice is yours."

Eleanor rested her hand on top of mine. "We need your decision by Wednesday. It'll be difficult to find a replacement at this time of year."

She and Halifax both stood to leave.

"Wait," I said.

They both stopped and looked at me, expectantly. And so they should have. I held all of the cards, and clearly, they needed me more than I needed them.

I said, "Sit."

They sat.

CHAPTER SIXTY

I closed my eyes and let my head fall back. If my eyes had been open, I would have been staring at the ceiling.

They weren't telling me everything. We were, of course, in the middle of a negotiation. They were selling me on staying by emphasizing the pros and downplaying the cons of staying, while emphasizing the cons and downplaying the pros of leaving. If Norbert were there, he'd do exactly the same, but from his perspective, to suit his agenda.

And then I did something I'd never done before.

Silently, I squeezed my right hand. On the one hand, I could take the new job.

I wriggled my right shoulder. What would I gain from taking the new job? An awesome and influential job.

I squeezed my left hand. On the other hand, I could stay.

I wriggled my left shoulder. If I stayed, then I'd possibly help save my friends' jobs. And for nine months I'd avoid an increased travel workload and get to spend more time with my family, which was good for them and for me.

I tipped my head slightly. The overarching need was my and my family's happiness.

I blinked my eyes open and searched for a moment for inspiration amongst the ceiling. I found none, so I closed my eyes again and summarized the conflict. I was torn between my own personal ambitions and the happiness of my friends and family.

This choice wasn't just about me.

Phil's advice to me long ago, that if you're jet lagged you might as well be eating bacon, did nothing for my mom or my kids, who bore the brunt of my travel.

I was sick of the travel. Bacon can't solve every problem.

Or can it?

Pigs don't just make good bacon, they also make good gifts—if you have a nice ribbon and know how to wrap it.

I opened my eyes. The new job's pig was clearly the increased travel. But what was the value of being "important" if my family suffered?

I smiled. I had the pig, and in that instant I figured out what the ribbon was. Now all I had to do was the wrapping.

I said, "We're only talking about nine months? And we're negotiating right now, correct?"

Hal and Eleanor both agreed. Eleanor was smiling hopefully, and Hal was doing his best to look neutral.

"Good." I pulled out my mobile and dialed Norbert's number, then switched it to speaker mode and rested it on the bench top.

"Hello, Steve. How did your launch go?"

"Great. We need to talk."

Saturday, November 18th
FPP is Live

CHAPTER SIXTY-ONE

I woke late the following morning, instantly regretting that I'd agreed to join Phil and Gregor and Vrinda and Tim and a half dozen others for just one pint after FPP's disco officially wrapped up last night.

Just one! Hah! Was there actually such a thing?

We'd started with a couple of pints of Guinness at The Burns Unit, then ambled down to High Street for an Indian, which we washed down with Kingfisher beer. Then, if I recall correctly, we fit in some black Russians before calling it an evening. I got a cab home sometime between midnight and sunrise and then slept until just after ten, when I finally forced myself out of bed, into the shower and down the stairs.

Alison was in the lounge watching cartoons under two dining chairs she had covered in rugs to make a den. I could hear Mum next door in the kitchen. Alison saw me and rushed over for hug. I crouched down—with difficulty—and told her I'd trade for a kiss. She leaned in and then, with the brutal honesty only a four-year-old girl can command, said, "Your breath stinks, Daddy."

I kissed her anyway, then tickled her to change the subject. "Where is Ashley?"

"Playing with friends out on the green."

"Did she take a jacket with her?"

"Maybe."

I screwed up my face. It was mid-November in Scotland, but

my kids and their friends seemed impervious to the cold, and in fact believed they had an inalienable right to bare arms.

"What you watching?"

"Scooby-Doo."

I glanced at the TV. "I've seen this one before. Is this the one where, right at the end, they discover the monster isn't really a monster, it's just someone dressed up like a monster?"

She looked at me and scrunched up her little nose. "Yeaah. They're all like that, Dad."

I went through to the kitchen. Mum was standing at the kitchen bench, her reading glasses on, doing The Times crossword.

She took one look at me, said, "My poor boy," and started preparing me a bacon sandwich, whether I wanted one or not.

While the bacon sizzled, she said, "You're far too old for these late nights."

"I got a promotion yesterday," I said, grinning despite myself. I had hoped to build up some tension and make a dramatic announcement, but I was just too excited to wait.

She smiled. "So you were celebrating?"

"Oh yes! Yesterday was maybe the best day of my career ever, Mom!"

"Do tell."

So I told. I stood there in the doorway of my tiny kitchen and told her the first part of my story while she stood at the counter, listening, turning the bacon and nodding in all the right places. I'd reached the bit where I called Norbert just as she finished slicing the finished sandwiches in half diagonally, which is how I liked them when I was a kid.

She popped the sandwiches on a plate and said, "Does this mean your travel is going to increase?" She looked pained by the thought.

"No."

"But you will have to travel after the summer next year?"

"No."

"No travel?" She looked confused. "Tell me then, clever clogs, how did you manage to get this promotion but not travel?"

I picked up my sandwich and took a tentative bite. The butter and the salt, the soft, soft bread and the crunch of the bacon, all mixed together with the ketchup's sharp sweetness were, at that moment, the best thing that had ever happened to me in my entire life. Ever.

"Mmmm. This is so good."

"Steven?"

I put the sandwich down, then smiled. "I brokered a deal between Norbert, Eleanor and Halifax. I will stay in Watt's Bridge, doing my utmost to ensure Future Perfect is a commercial success. As well as that, my team and I will use Wyx-Fin to figure out how to invert projects from the start. That's good for Wyx-Fin and for the Group."

She nodded. "It's good provided Future Perfect succeeds—but that isn't guaranteed."

"Future Perfect is my number one priority. But, assuming it goes well, then Norbert wants me to teach people in his other subsidiaries how to invert their projects. When that happens, I've told him that they can fork out for the airfares and fly to me. He's very happy with that."

She clapped her hands together. "Wonderful! Hal and Eleanor get what they want. You get the job you've always wanted. Norbert gets what he wants."

I looked out the window and noticed Alison and Ashley were playing together in the back yard. I watched them for a moment, then took another bite of my sandwich. I really did love the taste of bacon, but if I ever had to, I thought I could live without it.

I said, "And, best of all, I get to spend more time at home, with you and the kids."

She looked down at her hands, then back up to me. "Fran would be proud of you."

That was the best thing anyone could ever say to me.

THANK YOU FOR READING ROLLING ROCKS DOWNHILL

If you've enjoyed this book and you think others may find it valuable then please consider leaving a review on Amazon.com or Amazon.co.uk.

If you'd like to get an automatic update when I release the sequel, and other content, then please signup at http://www.rolls.rocks. I won't share your address with *anyone* and you can unsubscribe at any time. I will only ever contact you concerning new, useful, content. The story - clearly - isn't over yet.

Thank you for your time,

Clarke Ching, Linlithgow, Scotland.
clarke@rolls.rocks

ABOUT THE AUTHOR

Clarke Ching is an Agile and Theory of Constraints expert. Born in New Zealand, he now lives in Scotland with his wife, Winnie, and their two children, Aisling and Alice.

Made in the USA
Middletown, DE
21 June 2019